Cartoons

Introduction

Throughout this section of the book there are tips and advice on how to draw cartoons. There are suggestions for making up a cartoon story and ideas on how to keep a sketchbook. BUT the most important thing of all is to enjoy drawing.

Making a sketchbook

One of the best ways to get really good at drawing cartoons is to keep a sketchbook.

Observe – It is vital to look and listen to the world around you and record all the things you notice. This will be your store of ideas.

Key point – Always carry your sketchbook with you. Draw people, places, animals and buildings. Draw everything that interests you. It might be useful to jot down things that you overhear people say. This will help when you are thinking of a story.

Tip – Cut out pictures from OLD magazines, label and file them. Then when you need to draw a picture, you will have good references.

Making a Start

To draw cartoons you need a pencil, a scrap of paper, a good imagination and that's it. But if you want to gradually build up a stock of useful materials, here are some suggestions.

☆ **Tip**

Find a space where you can work. Make sure it has good light. Near a window is ideal. A drawing board isn't essential but it is good to have a clear table or desk. Maybe you can find a second-hand drawing board?

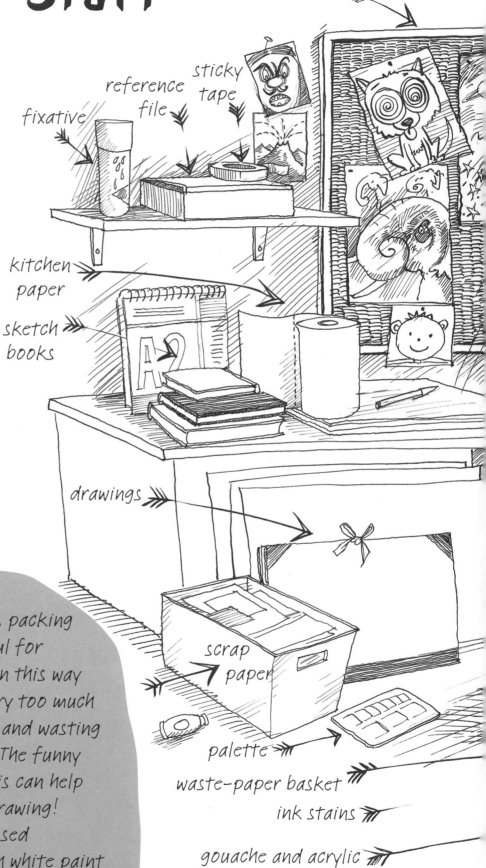

pin board
sticky tape
reference file
fixative
kitchen paper
sketch books
A2
drawings
scrap paper
palette
waste-paper basket
ink stains
gouache and acrylic
colouring pencils

📖 *Scrap deal*

A collection of old envelopes, packing and scrap paper is very useful for doodling. Using scrap paper in this way means you don't have to worry too much about a cartoon going wrong and wasting an expensive piece of paper. The funny thing is that just knowing this can help you make a really fabulous drawing!

You can always paint over used envelopes and packaging with white paint to give yourself a cleaner surface to draw on. Leave some writing showing through as this can look exciting.

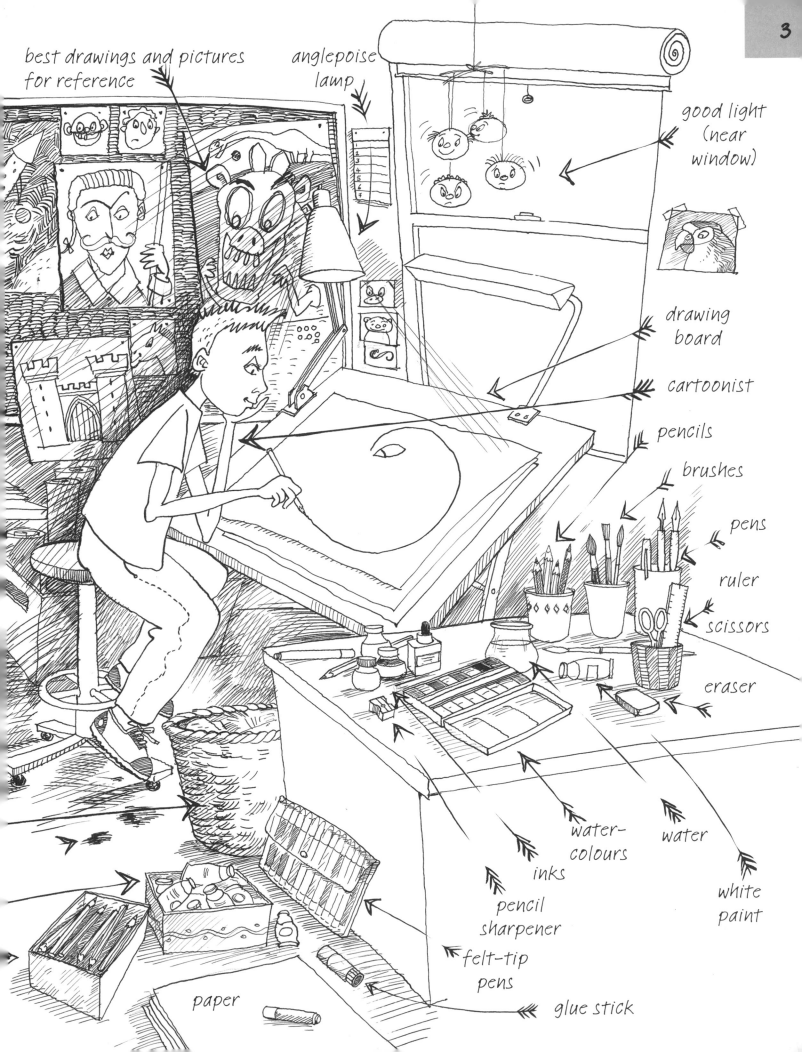

The Body

You will probably find it easier to start drawing your characters as pin-people.

★ **Tip**

Don't forget to draw in the hips and shoulders.

☞ **Key point**

Here the proportions are as in real life but with cartoon characters the heads are usually drawn much bigger. Try this! Now flesh out your pin-men starting with sausage shapes or, if you feel confident enough, try adding clothes straight away.

📖 *Body line up*

Practise drawing cartoon people in a variety of different poses in your sketchbook. Remember, the more you practise drawing, the better you will get.

⭐ **Tip**

Try emphasising your character's qualities.

For example, a thin, tall person could have a thin, tall head and a fat, round person could have a fat, round head.

👉 **Key point**

Notice how the stripes on these characters' shirts help to emphasise their shape.

Heads

A good way to start drawing cartoon heads is to reduce them to a simple shape like an oval or square.

 Shape

This is a basic shape for the head and can be used for many cartoon characters.

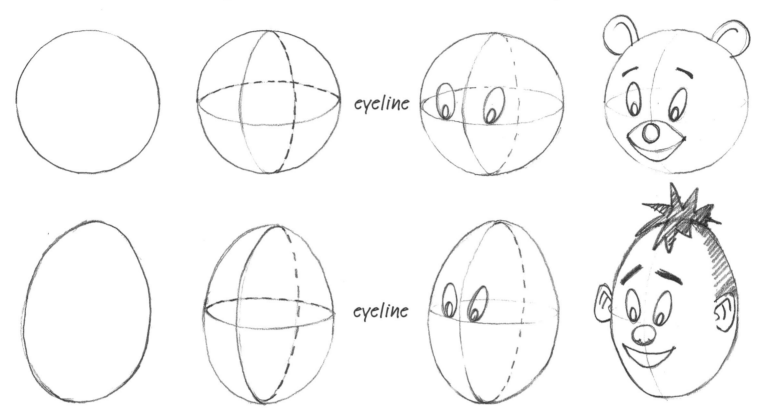

eyeline

eyeline

Draw a globe or an egg to start you off.

Divide this in half lengthways and note that the shape is 3D, not a flat circle or oval.

Draw in the eyeline which in real life would be roughly half of your globe but in cartoon life can be wherever you wish.

Now add the features.

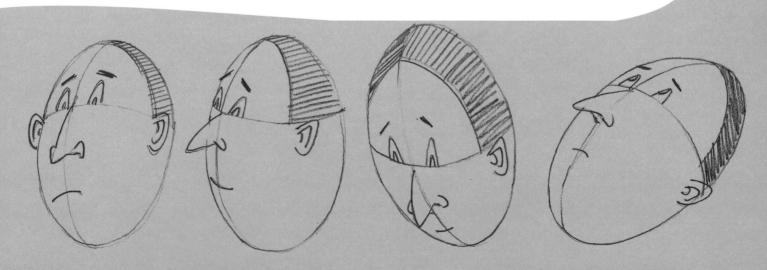

Key point

Notice how dramatically these faces change according to where in the shape their features are placed. With features at the top, our character has a large chin. When they are placed at the bottom, our character has a huge forehead! Experiment with this in your sketchbook.

Egg heads

Take an egg or table-tennis ball and draw on the two dividing lines – eyeline and lengthways – with a marker pen. Now draw your egg from many different viewpoints, looking up at it, down at it, sideways and so on. Add the features. This is great practice for drawing heads.

As your confidence grows, try making heads from different shapes.

Expressions

👁 Observe

Look at your own face in the mirror.
Like an actor, practise a range of different
expressions and try to draw them. Now pick
a character you can draw and try to match
his expression with a variety of different
emotions. For example, on this page I have
drawn a duchess character.

☞ Key point

Look at the opposite page. Notice how the
hair is used to reinforce the expression. It is
floppy and lank for 'tired', and jumping to
attention for 'frightened'.

Clothes and accessories can be used in the
same way to emphasise an emotion.
You can use body posture like this, too.

In this full-length portrait of the duchess, her
expression is one of surprise. Notice how her
earrings, handbag and tea cup are also caught
in mid-action. This adds to the feeling of
something having just happened. The white
streak in the duchess's hair imitates a question
mark.

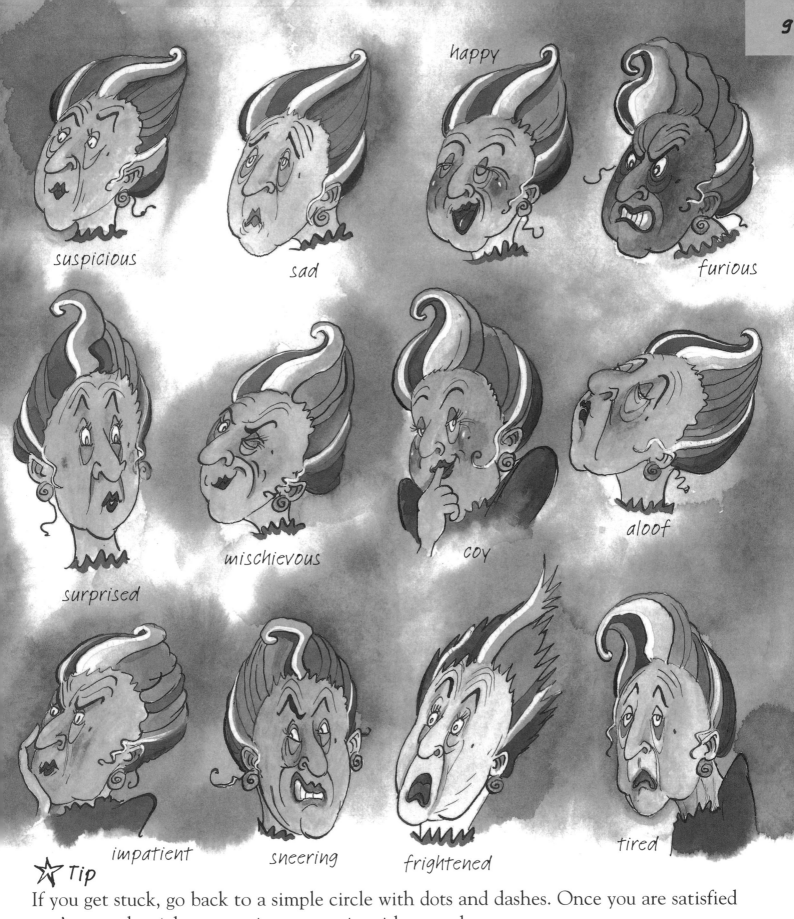

suspicious

sad

happy

furious

surprised

mischievous

coy

aloof

impatient

sneering

frightened

tired

⭐ Tip

If you get stuck, go back to a simple circle with dots and dashes. Once you are satisfied you've got the right expression, try again with your character.

Hands and Feet

Don't give up if you find drawing hands and feet difficult. They are! Even professional cartoonists find hands and feet difficult. Practise drawing from life as much as possible.

👁 Observe

For cartoon hands, don't attempt to draw all the lines on your hand. A few clear and simple marks will be easier to 'read'.

⭐ Tip

Your fingers are all different lengths. Look at your own hand.

Shape

Here are two ways to start drawing a hand:

1. Imagine the hand as a mitten. Then draw in the fingers.

2. Draw hands in the same way in which you might draw a pin-man - the bones first, then flesh out the drawing.

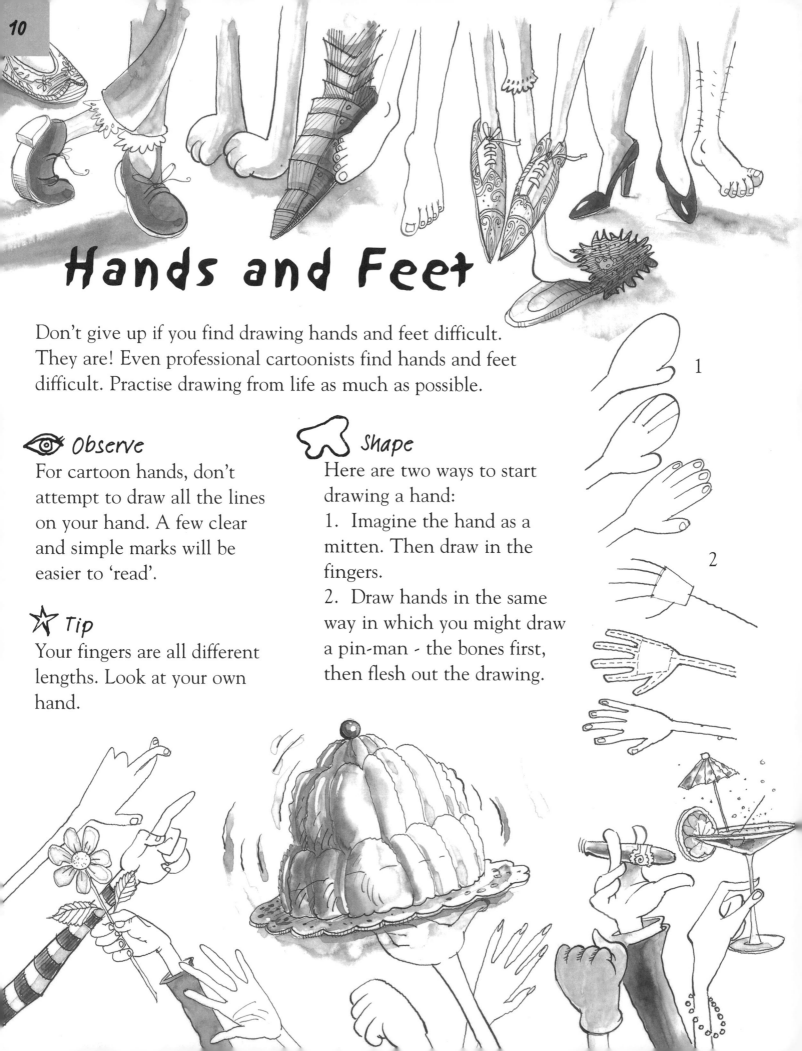

Key point

You can tell a lot about the character from the type of shoes they wear. So think carefully before dressing your cartoon characters. Their shoes may be dirty or extra shiny, big or small.

Well shod

Start a shoe sketchbook and fill it with drawings of people's shoes. Draw the shoes on and off the foot. If possible, make a rubbing or print of the shoe tread pattern as well.

Moving On

When drawing cartoon characters, ANYTHING GOES!

 *Observe*

Look at these simple characters. They are just like pin-men that have been filled out. Their facial features (eyes, nose) can be made up with dots and dashes or circles within circles.
You can practise by drawing these characters.
If you get stuck, turn back to the pin-man page.

Here the characters are walking, then running. For really fast running you can use speed lines like I've done or even add words like 'Whoosh' and 'Zoom'. They can be any colour and any shape, so use your imagination and create some really exciting characters.

☆ *Tip*
For extra speed, draw your character running with his feet not touching the ground.

Cast of Characters

In the world of cartoon characters, stereotypes rule. A cartoon artist will probably wear a floppy hat, a smock, and hold an artist's palette with brushes. A real artist wouldn't walk around dressed like this but in cartoons you need to be able to identify the character quickly.

Here is a cast of characters for you to copy.

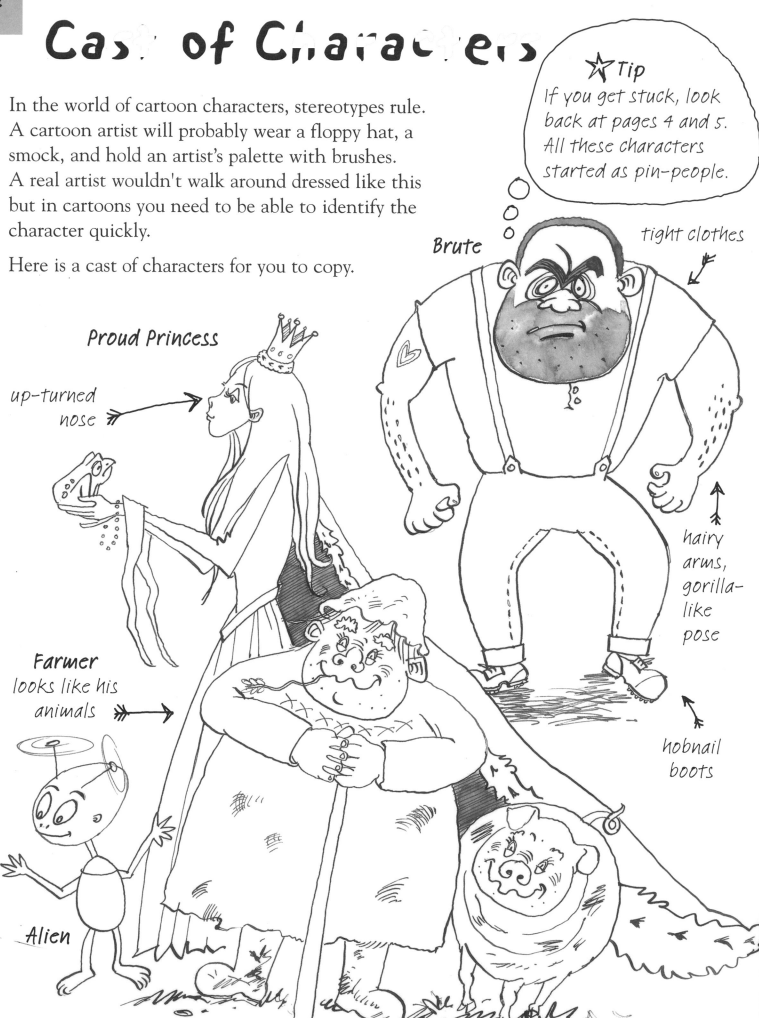

★ Tip
If you get stuck, look back at pages 4 and 5. All these characters started as pin-people.

Brute

tight clothes

Proud Princess

up-turned nose

hairy arms, gorilla-like pose

hobnail boots

Farmer
looks like his animals

Alien

Mad Professor

large forehead for big brain

bow tie

white coat

check trousers

odd socks

Wacky Witch

long finger nails

warts on nose

book of spells

bloomers

Old Woman

twinkly eyes

saucer of milk for puss

📖 *Rogues' gallery*
As you gain confidence, try creating your own characters. Draw them in different positions and doing different things. Here are some more suggestions: Cut-throat Pirate, Circus Clown, Pop Idol, Film Star, School Cook.

Machines

You can make a cartoon character from anything, including machines.

Shape

To draw a car, start with
two rectangles. Add the wheels,
the doors and all of the details
like the lights and bumpers.
This is a good basis for any car.
For a fast car, make the shape long and thin.
For a slow car, tall and square is best.

☆ Tip

Use speed lines and angle the wheels to give
an impression of speed.

Observe

Here I've given this car a face by changing the headlights and radiator to eyes and a toothy grin. It's great fun to animate machines in this way and almost any machine can be given this treatment.

Mad machines

Visit a transport or science museum with your sketchbook. Draw the machines and, if you have a camera, take some photographs. At home, try turning your drawings into cartoon characters.

Cartoon Animals

You can usually start drawing cartoon animals with a simple shape like a circle, oval or triangle.

👁 Observe

Start the drawing of the dog with a circle for the head and an oval for the body. Finish this first stage with lines for legs and smaller circles for feet.

Shape

Gradually flesh out your drawing adding the ears, nose, eyes and tail. Finally, add any markings.

⭐ Tip

Remember, in cartoon world anything goes: your dog may walk on two legs; it may be orange, blue or purple; it may even ride a bike.

Dog

Cat

Bird

Mouse

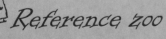 Reference zoo

Start a collection of animal pictures.
Cut out pictures from magazines or, better still, draw animals from real life in your sketchbook. After a while you will have a useful reference book to use as a source for your cartoons.

Here is a page of cartoon animals. Copy them and let them inspire you to make up your own characters. Once you can draw your cartoon character, try drawing it with different expressions.

⭐ *Tip*
The patterns on an animal's body often help to show the shape.

Foreground

Once you are confident in drawing cartoon characters, you can set them in a scene or 'frame' and make a picture.

You can roughly break a picture into three separate areas or planes: the foreground, the middle ground and the background.

👁 Observe

The foreground means what is in front and, therefore, closest to us. You can use it to create drama and atmosphere and to show close-up expressions. The examples on this page show how to use the foreground.

☝ Key point

The foreground is very useful in cartoons to show emotions or surprise. The sudden 'cut' to a close-up makes the most of this dramatic moment.

☆ Tip

When making up the pictures in a story, don't overuse the foreground. An occasional close-up is much more effective.

Middle Ground

The middle ground is the most used of our three planes.
It is usually where the action takes place.
Here are some examples of how you might use the middle ground.

Setting the scene

Try making a simple concertina. Draw the background, side pieces and proscenium to slot or stick in (see below). This is like a mini theatre and you can play with the background, middle ground and foreground and maybe draw some characters. Finally, try making drawings from the model in your sketchbook.

Background

Background is important for setting the scene and for showing where the action is taking place.

👁 *Observe*

Look at these drawings of a pin-man in the desert.
Notice how in (a) we feel that the pin-man is just setting out on his journey.
In (b) and (c) we guess that he is in the middle of the desert as the background seems to go on and on. But in (d) the feeling is that he is near the end and coming out of the desert. The only thing that is different in all of these boxes is the horizon line.

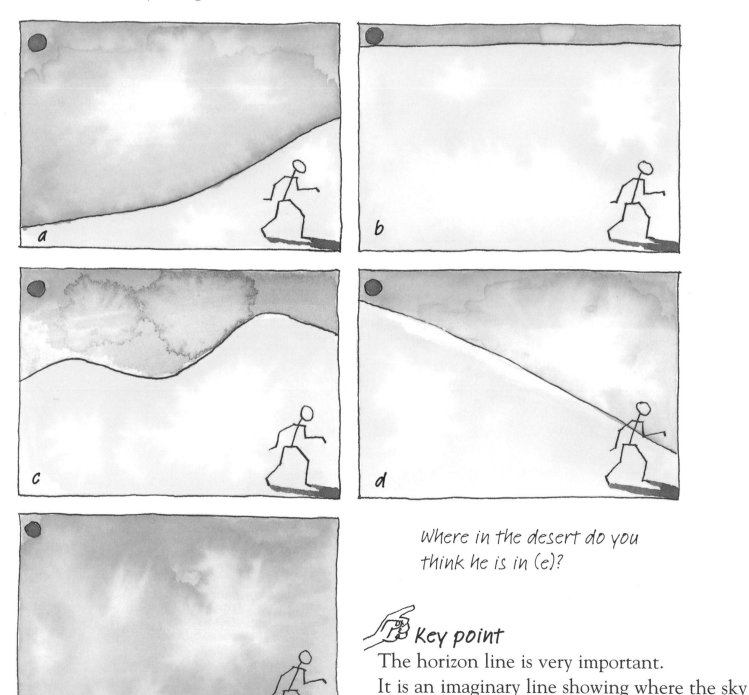

Where in the desert do you think he is in (e)?

👉 *Key point*

The horizon line is very important.
It is an imaginary line showing where the sky joins the land. It can dramatically alter the mood and meaning of your cartoons.

Observe

The background in this frame is important to set the scene for this story. The distant mountains, fields and path stretching from the house really help give the picture depth.

Key point

Notice how the use of the foreground in all these pictures adds to the atmosphere.

In all of these examples, notice how the three planes work together to create a great picture, full of atmosphere and drama.

Field trip

Take a trip to an art gallery and look at the paintings. How are the middle ground and background used in pictures? Try recording in your sketchbook those you find most interesting. You can do the same thing watching films on TV. How do directors make their compositions exciting?

Comic Strips

The first thing you need is a story and this should be exciting or funny or maybe both. Don't make it too long or you won't leave enough room for the pictures.

Here are some suggestions for comic-strip stories. You can use these or make up your own.

BIG DOG - Alice's family buy a puppy but it cannot stop growing and growing and growing...

THE SEA SHELL GIRL - on holiday Pearl finds a sea shell but, as she discovers when her family return home, inside lives a tiny mermaid who must return to the sea.

AUNT RAT - Emily's aunt has a special trick. She can turn herself into a rat!

FLYING LENNY - Lenny wakes up to find he can fly.

THE VOYAGE OF THE EMERALD TIGER - Oliver stows away on board *The Emerald Tiger* as it sails in search of treasure and adventure.

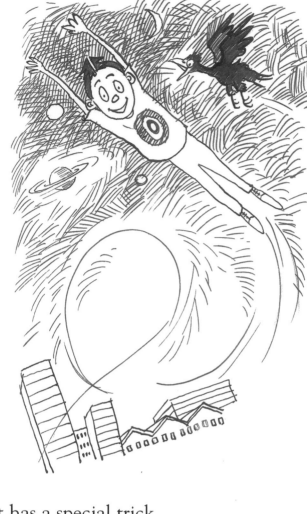

Once you have the plot, you can create the characters. Practise drawing them in your sketchbook over and over again.

⭐ Tip
You will need to make your characters look the same in each frame, so keep their features simple.

👉 Key point
Do the comic strip in pencil first. Put in all of the speech bubbles. This is a great way to make sure everything fits and to deal with any problems before you spend ages on the finished comic strip. This is called a 'rough' or 'visual' and nearly all illustrators and cartoonists work like this.

Make your frames different sizes. It's more interesting. Look back at the pages on foreground, middle ground and background.

Four hours later...

A sentence at the top of the frame can tell you the time or place, e.g. 'Four hours later...' or, 'Meanwhile, back at the ranch.'

Frisky! Get down.

Oh no!

This looks fun!

It is easier to do the lettering first and draw the speech bubbles around after. Remember to put the speech bubbles in the order you want them to be read – from left to right. This is important because it may dictate where your characters need to be. You can use thought bubbles as well as speech bubbles.

Draw the frame outlines with a ruler and pencil first BUT then draw over this guide in freehand.

BANG!

snooze zzzzzz

Sound effects are a great way of making your story come alive.

Look at how all these are used in the story on the next page.

Caricature

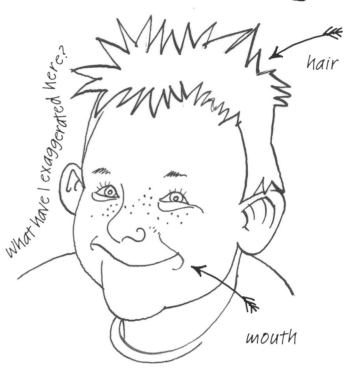

What have I exaggerated here?

hair

mouth

Making a caricature of someone is all about looking.
Look for a dominant feature that you can exaggerate, maybe a nose or eyebrows.

 Key point

It is important that any information in your cartoon is understood clearly and quickly. To achieve this, simplify your drawings down to just the essential details. This way the reader can see instantly what you wish to communicate.

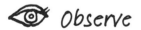 **Observe**

Here I have caricatured a family friend as a Bassett hound! I did this, not only because her hair reminds me of a dog's ears but she actually owns two Bassett hounds. Look for chances like this when you are thinking how to caricature someone.

👁 Observe

Look and think carefully about the person you are caricaturing. Do they usually wear the same kind of thing or a particular colour? If so, dressing them in this will really help. Do they have a mannerism or habit you could include? They might like skateboarding so draw them with a skateboard or if they love music, draw them with headphones and musical notes.

Here are some examples of caricatures. What do they tell you about the 'victim'?

⭐ Tip

Maybe you could draw them doing a favourite activity or job. Can you guess which of these is me?

📖 Mug shots!

Try caricaturing your family and friends, then test them on other members of your family to see if they know who it is. Tone down the exaggeration if they cannot tell who it is.

Top Ten Tips

⭐ Always carry your sketchbook and draw at every available opportunity.

⭐ Don't try to fit too much into each picture.

⭐ Look at your own face in the mirror to capture the expression you want.

⭐ Written sound effects can help to tell a story.

⭐ Always start with a thumbnail sketch before spending time on a larger finished drawing.

⭐ The simpler an image, the easier it will be to understand.

⭐ Keep scraps of paper to draw on. Sometimes the best drawings are made on the backs of envelopes.

⭐ Pin-people are a good way to start drawing cartoon figures.

⭐ If you are having trouble drawing something, look at the real thing.

⭐ When using speech bubbles, remember to leave enough space for the words.

Horses

Introduction

This section is about horses and how to draw them. You can draw them from life at the stables, from reference at home, or even straight from your imagination. It doesn't matter as long as you are drawing and enjoying it.

Making a start

The first thing to do is to try and see a real horse. Maybe you have a riding stables near you that you could visit or maybe there is an urban farm or a field with horses in. It will make a tremendous difference just looking at the real thing.

Horse box

Start a collection of horse photographs. Cut them out of magazines and newspapers and store them in a box or book. This will be the beginning of your reference library.

Step by step Horses

To draw horses well, it is essential to draw one from life. Then you can observe closely how a horse moves and behaves. It might help to get to know your subject a little first and that is really the idea behind these drawings.

👁 Observe

Look at these step-by-step drawings and try copying them, gradually building up a complete drawing of a horse. I started with two ovals, a large one for the body and a small one for the head. Then flesh out the neck and legs from your initial lines and add the details last.

⭐ Tip

If you struggle with a particular part of the body, like the ears or head, make separate studies of these until you feel confident.

lined paper

ADVENTURE

packaging

brown paper

ink stain

tracing paper

old book
lightly painted over
with white

On the hoof

If you want to become good at drawing horses,
or anything else, then it is vital to keep a sketchbook.
You can make this by clipping some paper together or you can buy
one. Take your sketchbook with you wherever you go and draw what
you see. Start with a collection of drawings of horses' hooves.
Copy from paintings, photographs and from life. Look at your
reference box (page 33). You'll soon know how to draw them.

☆ Tip

An excellent idea is to prepare each sketchbook double page with
a surface or background. You'll find these great fun to draw on
and drawing tools will respond in different ways to these surfaces,
so experiment to find successful combinations. There are some
suggestions on this page, and more tips throughout the book.

magazines
lightly painted
over with white

More Step by Step Horses

Here are two more pages of step-by-step horses to help you to practise.

As your confidence grows, try leaving out some of the simple earlier stages.

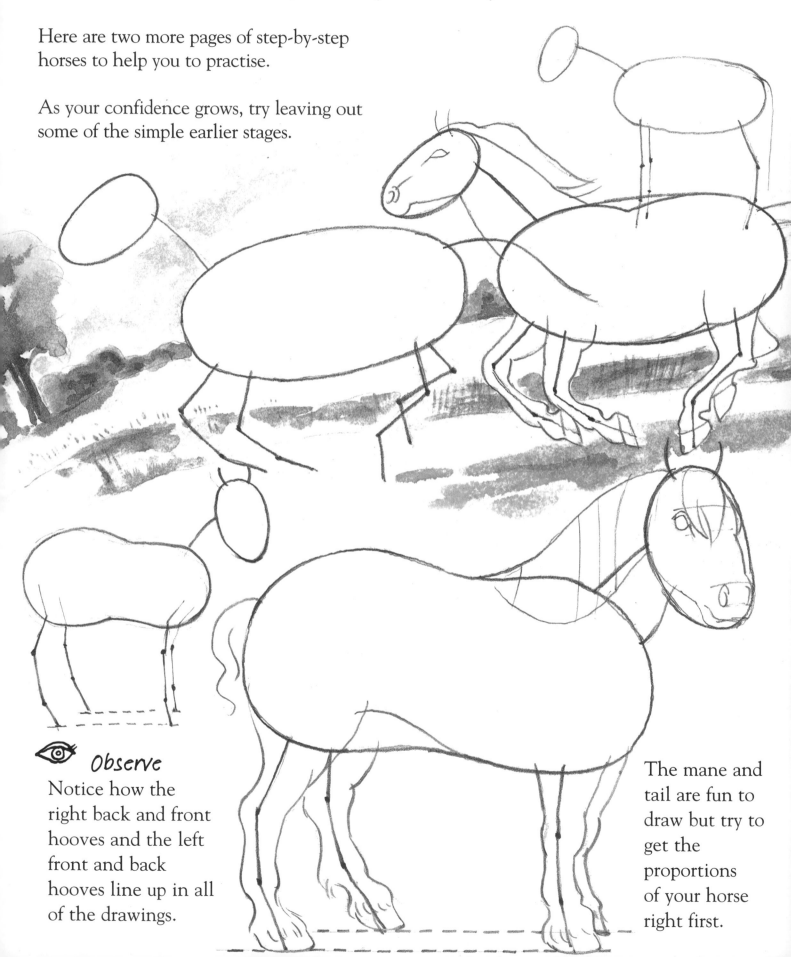

👁 *Observe*
Notice how the right back and front hooves and the left front and back hooves line up in all of the drawings.

The mane and tail are fun to draw but try to get the proportions of your horse right first.

Aim to be adventurous when you work on your drawings. Try as many different tools as you can so you get to know how each works and what effect you can achieve with it.

⭐ Tip
Pencils range from 6H, the hardest, to 6B, the softest, with HB exactly in the middle. A soft pencil lets you blur the line and is ideal for thick, expressive strokes but try not to make your drawing woolly. Never use anything harder than an HB to draw like this with.

You can add tones (shading) either by using an ordinary pencil, or a water-soluble pencil like an Aquarelle, by running a wet brush over the line as in the drawing (left) of the heavy horse.

Horses at Home

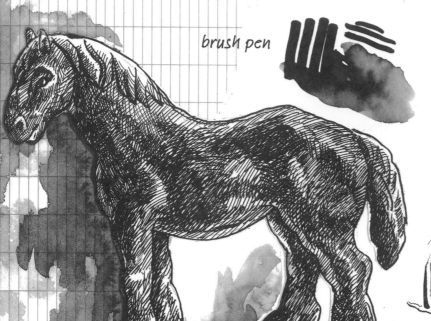

brush pen

These drawings were made from a toy model horse. This is excellent practice and will give you a real idea of the shape, proportions and anatomy of a horse before you attempt to draw a real one from life. You can buy them from most toy shops.

dip pen

fibre-tip pen

Drawing tool

This drawing was made with a fibre-tip pen. The shading is made by cross-hatching. A limitation of this pen is that the line is always the same thickness. Compare the marks of the fibre-tip pen and those of the dip pen.

fountain pen

👁 Observe

The detail on these toy models is often superb, so look closely while you draw.

Model pupil

Try building up a collection of drawings from models; maybe make a series of small books, one for each model. This kind of drawing is called 'observational drawing'. It is excellent practice to look at something three-dimensional and try to keep this solidity in your two-dimensional drawing.

Drawing tool
These drawings were made using a fountain pen (see page 44).

Key point
I have made a drawing from every angle of this model, turning it round a little more each time and starting again.

Heads

If you make detailed studies of all parts of the horse's body, this will help you to understand exactly what it looks like. Here are two pages of heads to copy. A horse is symmetrical in shape so this is a big help.

gift wrap painted over with white

⭐ **Tip**
Try drawing half a horse's head on a piece of paper with paint. If you are quick and fold the paper over before the paint is dry, the other half of your horse's head will print. This shows it is symmetrical.

brown paper

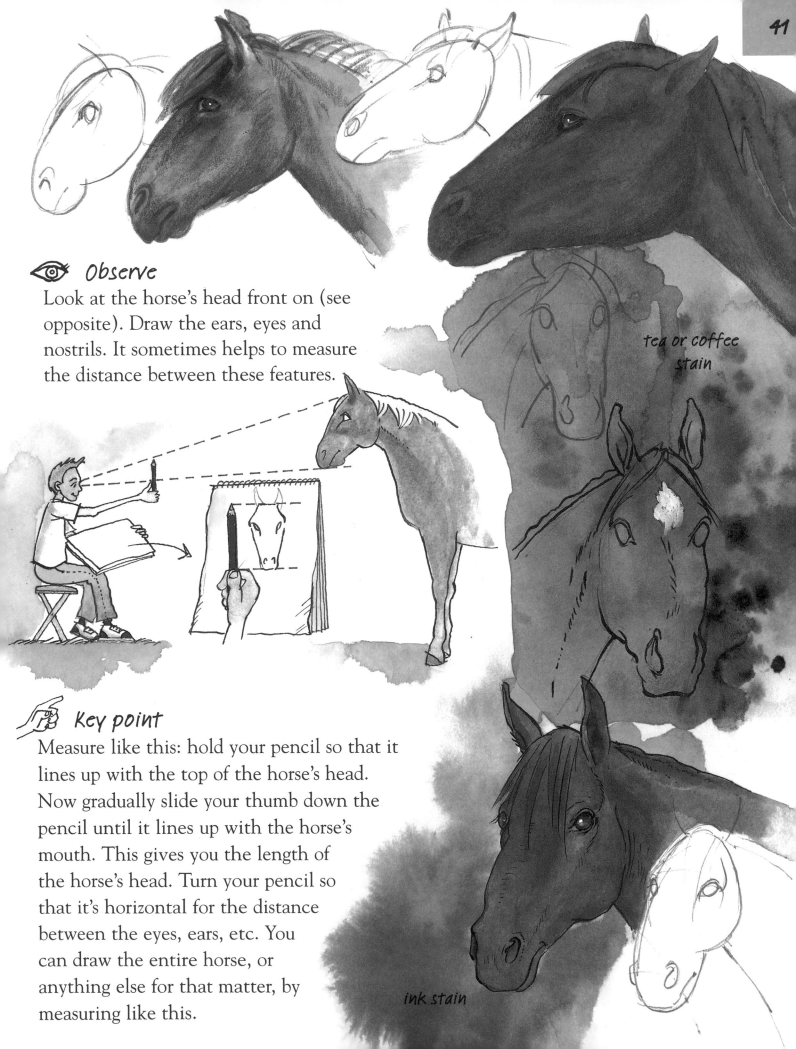

👁 Observe

Look at the horse's head front on (see opposite). Draw the ears, eyes and nostrils. It sometimes helps to measure the distance between these features.

tea or coffee stain

✍ Key point

Measure like this: hold your pencil so that it lines up with the top of the horse's head. Now gradually slide your thumb down the pencil until it lines up with the horse's mouth. This gives you the length of the horse's head. Turn your pencil so that it's horizontal for the distance between the eyes, ears, etc. You can draw the entire horse, or anything else for that matter, by measuring like this.

ink stain

Drawing from Photographs

It is always better to draw from the living animal but if this isn't possible, a good quality photograph is second best.

Key point

Firstly, make sure it is a good quality photograph that shows plenty of detail.

Tip

Try making several drawings from one photograph using different drawing tools. Compare your drawings and try to analyse which works best and why.

Drawing tool

For the drawing of this pony, I used a mixture of different media: ink, pencil, watercolour, and gouache (paint). It helps to make this drawing really exciting and alive.

Photo fit
If you have a camera it is a good idea to take a photograph of the horse you are drawing from life. You can refer to this later at home. Write on the back where you drew the horse and any other information you can find out, like what breed it is, its name and how old it is.

Tip
To help to keep your drawing lively, try looking at the photograph for a few minutes. Then turn it over and draw from memory.

Key point
Remember that the horse is a living three-dimensional animal, not a two-dimensional cut-out so try to make your drawing solid.

At the Stables

A great way to study horses close up is to visit a riding stables. Check that the stable owners don't mind you drawing there and go well prepared. Take your sketchbook and maybe even some larger paper. Take a varied selection of drawing tools and wear something warm. When you sit drawing for a long time outside you'll be surprised how cold you can get even on a sunny day.

Drawing tool

Here I've used a fountain pen to draw with. It is excellent for taking on location. It doesn't dry up, you can smudge the ink with water and it easily fits in your pocket.

☝ Key point

Try to begin a drawing within five minutes of arriving. If you spend too much time wandering around thinking about what to draw, you could end up doing nothing. If you start quickly you are much more likely to have a successful day. The more you draw, the easier it will be.

☆ Tip

It is best to choose just one horse and draw it many times. Then you'll get to know it and your drawings will improve.

Never sit closely behind a horse. Sit where it can see you and be careful not to startle it with sudden movements or noises such as turning over large sheets of paper. Horses' temperaments vary just like ours and the stable owner will probably tell you which horse will not like being drawn.

Drawing from Life

When you draw from life, it is unlikely that you will end up with one complete drawing of a horse. More usual will be pages of drawings of heads, bodies, feet all half started and jumbled together. As you can see on these two pages, the drawings I made of horses in a field are just like that. But all the information I need to draw a completed horse is here.

☆ Tip

Make written notes as well as drawings. Try to record colour. Use arrows to point to details that are repeated rather than draw them over and over again.

Horses for courses

You will only find out which drawing tool is best for the job by experimenting. Try them out in your sketchbook. Here are some tips on drawing tools and what they might do.

Charcoal. Use the side for thick, broad areas of shading and the tip for drawing. Charcoal will give a huge range of tones from deepest black to pale, pale grey but your drawing will need fixing to stop it smudging. You can buy fixative or use hairspray.

Fibre-tip pen. Clean and easy to use, best for drawing on location where too many materials would be impractical (see page 38).

Dip pen. Fabulous for lively drawings but you will need practice. You will also need to carry a bottle of Indian ink which you should dilute with distilled water.

Ball point. Great for quick drawings in difficult, busy locations.

Wax crayon. Best for large drawings as it is difficult to draw small details with wax crayons.

Marker pen. I like to use these when they are running out as they make a more varied mark. Again better for quite big drawings.

Cartoon Horses

Here are a few tips on how to draw cartoon horses. You can adapt some of your drawings or just draw straight from your head. To draw a cartoon horse you exaggerate and play with the characteristics of a real horse.

Observe

Start with an oval and a circle for the body and head. Follow these step-by-step stages and gradually flesh out your drawing.

Mind my eye.

Personalised ponies

Make a greetings card using some of your cartoon drawings. If you can think of a joke you can include this or maybe make something like a good-luck card in a horse-shoe shape. Here are some suggestions for headings to get you thinking: Pony Post! Riding High! First past the Post!

Key point

In the cartoon world anything goes, so your horse can walk on two legs or drive a car, or it can be pink with a blue mane. Let your imagination go into overdrive.

Horses in Action

To draw horses in action, try to freeze the image in your memory and then quickly draw it. It really helps to use something like a brush dipped in ink or a stick of charcoal because this is not about drawing detail but about capturing a moment on paper. This is very difficult and you'll probably find it easier to start by copying photographs.

Key point
Don't worry if you find this difficult. It is. Don't give up. Your hand and eye co-ordination skills will soon improve with practice.

Observe
Notice how the background behind this horse is blurred. This adds to the feeling of movement and energy.

☆ **Tip**

To try to capture the life and energy of the real thing
I've used a stick dipped in ink.

Sketchbook activity

The key to success with drawing horses in action is to spend more
time looking at the horse and less time looking at the paper.
Practise drawing your model horses without looking at the paper.
DON'T CHEAT! You'll soon get used to not looking at your drawing
and with luck everything will be more or less in the right place.

Horses in Art

The horse was domesticated about six thousand years ago and Man has continually represented it in paintings, drawings and sculptures. There are images of horses on Greek pots, Viking tapestries, and cave paintings in Spain that date back seventeen thousand years.

Painted ponies

We can learn a lot by looking at and recording images of horses from past civilisations. Visit a museum or an art gallery with your sketchbook. Make copies of as many horses as you can. Try to record the colours and patterns. Observe how the harnesses change over time. You'll soon fill up a sketchbook.

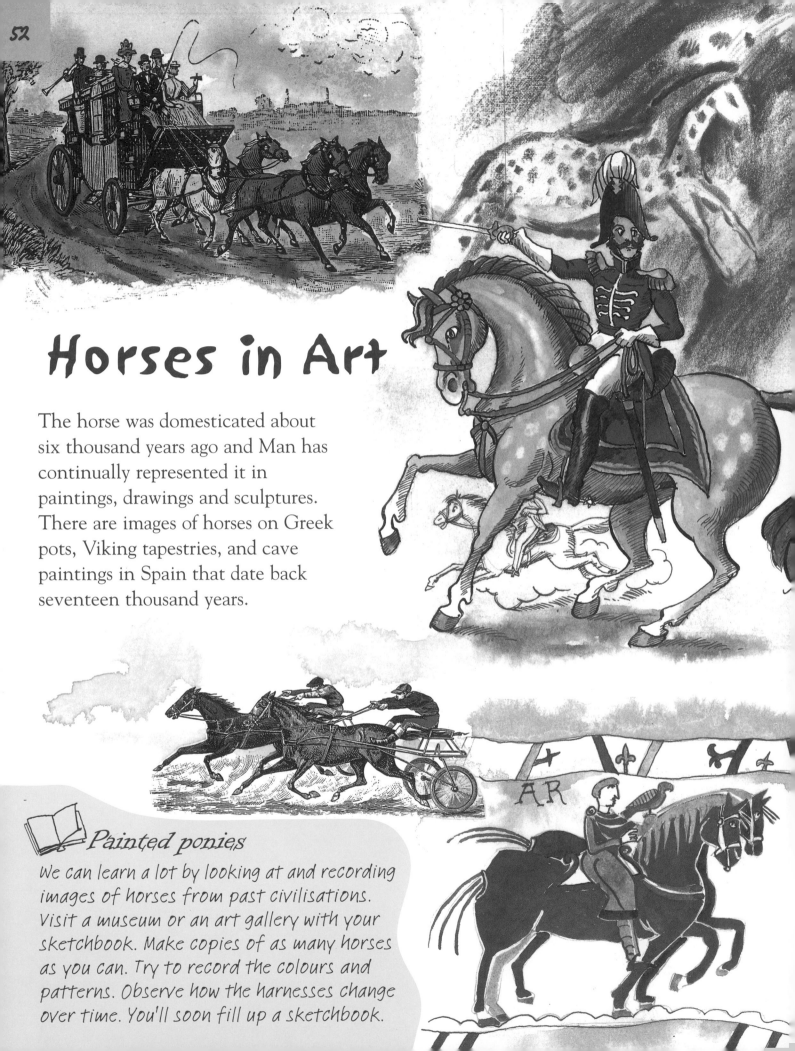

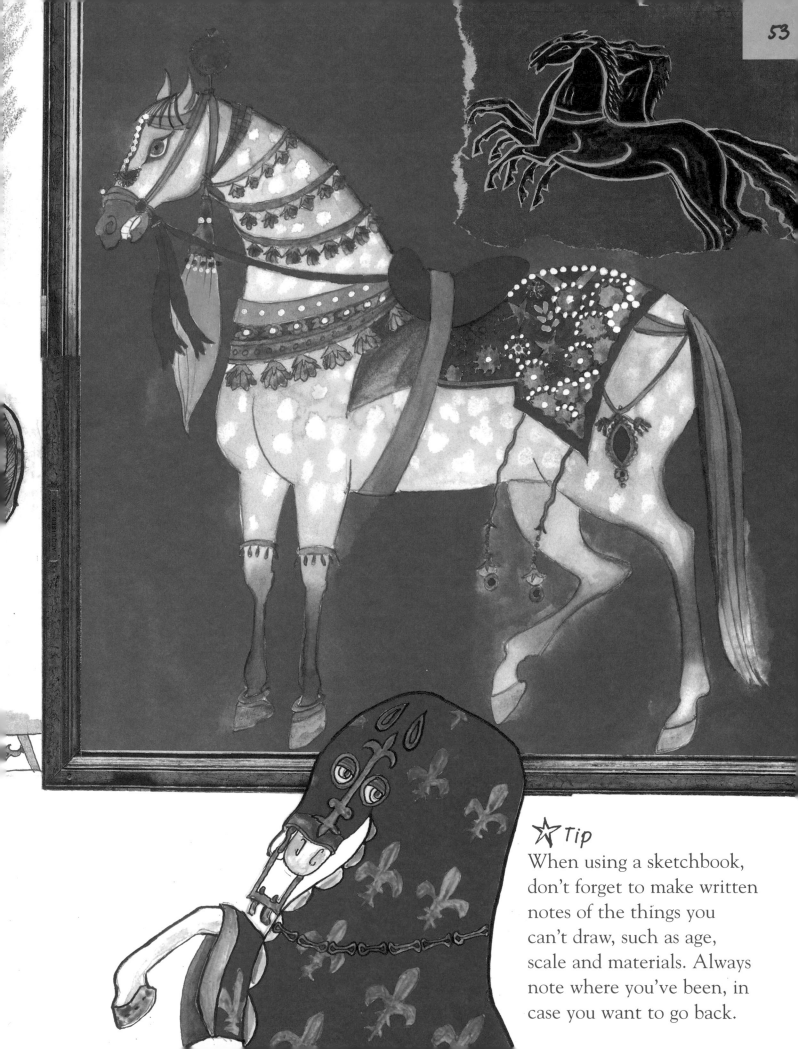

☆*Tip*
When using a sketchbook,
don't forget to make written
notes of the things you
can't draw, such as age,
scale and materials. Always
note where you've been, in
case you want to go back.

Foals

If you are lucky enough to see a foal, don't miss the chance to draw it.

👁 *Observe*

In all of these drawings, start with a larger oval for the body and a smaller oval for the head. Then draw in the neck and legs. Look closely to get the proportions correct. Use lines first, then flesh them out. Add the short tail and upright mane with the final details.

⭐ *Tip*

Look at the proportions. It is the length of a foal's legs that give it that characteristic gangly look.

Key point

A foal's head is short in length and the nose is slightly rounded. The tail is curly and the mane stands up like a brush. If you look carefully and observe these details, your drawing will soon improve.

Breeds

Here is a range of different breeds for you to copy. Look carefully at the differences between them.

Shire

The Shire horse is descended from the medieval war horse. It is a giant breed, strong enough to carry a knight in full armour.

 Shire silhouettes

Draw an outline of a Shire horse on a piece of card and carefully cut it out. You can either use the card as a stencil and dab paint through to make an image or you can spray paint around the cut-out piece. You can even paint the cut-out piece to use as a simple print. Try making gift wrap or greetings cards with your Shire silhouettes.

👁 *Observe*

The 'feather' on the feet and the massive build are both important features of the Shire horse.

Arab

A beautiful horse. The eyes and the nostrils are large and the face is slightly dipped. These details are important and will help make your drawing recognisable.

Palomino

With its white mane and golden-coloured body, the Palomino is very striking. It is all about colour so it is important to get this right.

Tack

The equipment used for riding horses is usually called 'tack'.

bridle

halter

head collar

These drawings show some of the more common pieces of tack.
You will come across these when you draw horses, so if you know exactly how they fit on the horse, this will help when you draw them. Tack varies a lot, so always draw what you see.

saddle

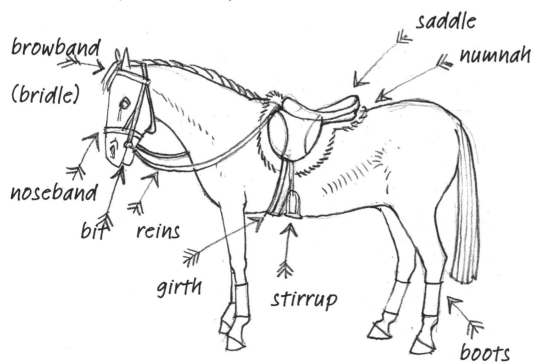

browband
(bridle)

noseband

bit   reins

girth   stirrup

boots

saddle
numnah

The tack on the horse opposite, taken from a heraldic crest, is several hundred years old but has changed little from modern tack.
The strap around the top of its front legs is called a 'martingale'. It is to stop the horse raising its head too high.

Heraldic Horses

Horses and unicorns are frequently used in
heraldry and appear on crests, shields and
coats of arms. They are used as logos for banks,
cars, building societies and fashion houses.
They are embossed on coins and stylised as
figures in games like chess. Start a collection
of drawings, rubbings and prints of heraldic
horses. The dramatic and exaggerated nature
of the horses in heraldry with their prancing
legs and rearing posture make exciting
subjects. They work especially well on
sketchbook pages that have been prepared
with patches of bright, strong colour.

Mythical Horses

Horses abound in mythology and you may feel inspired to create pictures of legendary horses like unicorns and the winged Pegasus. Let your imagination take over. The important thing in creating images like this isn't drawing the leg exactly right but whether or not the drawing is exciting and dramatic.

Pegasus

According to Greek mythology, this famous winged horse was ridden by Bellerophon in his epic battle with the Chimaera monster.

👁 Observe

It is his wings that make this drawing so exciting. Study some stuffed birds in a museum and practise drawing them to get the wings right.

👉 Key point

The wings need to be drawn big because they have a lot to carry. If the wings are too small, the drawing will look unconvincing even though it is a mythical beast.

Sleipnir

According to Norse mythology, Sleipnir was a grey colt with eight legs who galloped around the heavens (Valhalla), carrying mighty Odin on his back.

✍ Key point

The background for both of these horses is very important in setting the scene.

★ Tip

Don't be afraid to have a go at drawings like these. The basic form is still just a horse. Go back to the step-by-step drawings on page 34 if necessary.

Horse and Rider

Here are some drawings of a horse and rider together. Use the step-by-step drawings to get the idea of how these two 'fit' together. It is difficult so don't expect instant success.

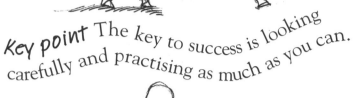

Key point The key to success is looking carefully and practising as much as you can.

Show off

If you can visit a horse show or a gymkhana, take your sketchbook with you. You can usually find these events listed in a local paper or ask the Pony Club (an international organisation with local branches: www.pcuk.org). Prepare your sketchbook first. Take a fountain pen if possible as it will not dry up whilst you are waiting for a horse and rider to come into view and the ink can be smudged to make a thicker line. The fountain pen can also make very varied marks and will fit easily into your pocket, so all in all it is an excellent choice for location drawing.

☆ **Tip**

Don't worry about mistakes, just draw what you can. Here are some ideas for correcting your drawings if necessary.

line erased

white paint

patch

There are several ways to alter a drawing. Here are some of the methods artists use:

- You can rub out. Draw the 'new' correct line before you erase the old one.
- You can use white paint to cover up unwanted lines.
- You can stick a patch of paper over a messy area.

Top Ten Tips

⭐ Study a real horse before trying to draw one.

⭐ Measure with your thumb and a pencil to help you to get the proportions right.

⭐ Use a variety of drawing tools, not just a pencil.

⭐ Draw with a brush or stick of charcoal to add life to your drawing.

⭐ Use a fountain pen when drawing on location.

⭐ When visiting a location, try to begin a drawing within five minutes.

⭐ Try to look at what you are drawing, not at the paper.

⭐ When using a sketchbook, don't forget to make written notes.

⭐ Lots of practice will improve your drawing.

⭐ Most of all, enjoy your drawing.

GOOD LUCK!

Monsters

Introduction

This section is all about monsters! It's all about how to create them, draw and paint them. There are step-by-step drawings to help you and projects to do in a sketchbook. (Look out for the special sketchbook symbol below.) There are tips and advice on how to make your monsters scary, funny, friendly or fierce. But don't forget that the most important thing is to enjoy drawing.

Keeping a sketchbook

It's very important to keep a sketchbook. Always carry it with you so you can draw things you notice in the world around you and make written notes.

You can buy a sketchbook or make one by clipping pieces of paper together. It is a good idea to prepare the pages. Paint or stain each double page with a background wash of ink or watercolour. You can also line it with other paper, like brown paper or wallpaper. Look at the examples below. Make notes on how different drawing tools, pencil, pen, crayon or paint, respond to each surface.

wallpaper

brown paper

Patches of colour (not too bright)

Packaging and magazines partly covered with white

map

lining paper

tissue

newspaper

Real life Monsters

There is no substitute for looking at the real thing and trying to draw it. But you cannot very well go out and ask a monster to pose for you. However, you can draw real creatures that sometimes seem scary, like spiders, snakes, beetles and bats. This will be very useful when you are making up imaginary monsters.

Spiders

House spiders look fearsome but are, in fact, completely harmless. Catch them gently in a glass or jar. Draw them and then release them.

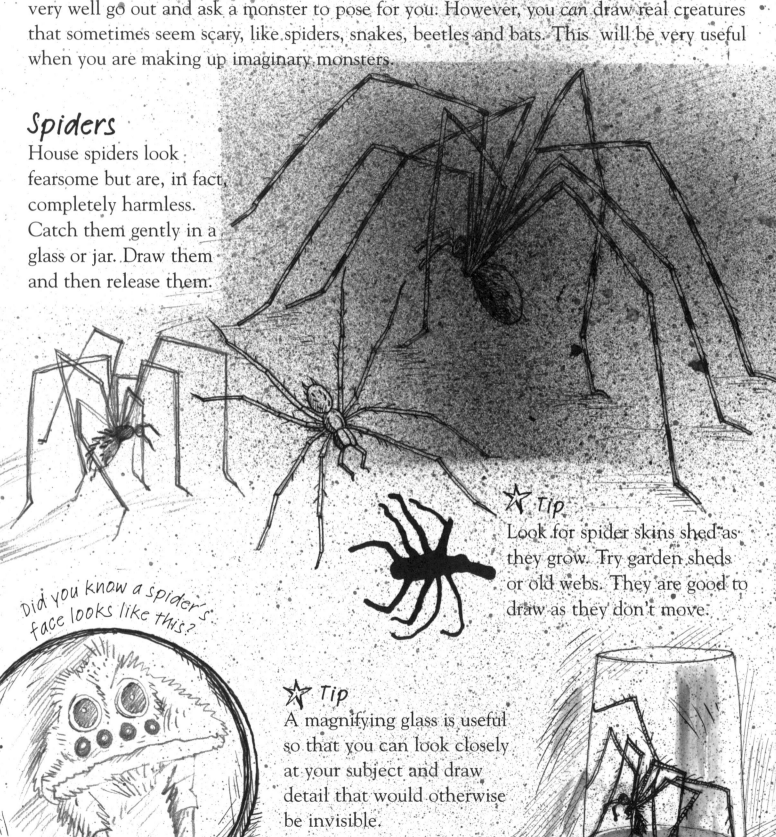

Did you know a spider's face looks like this?

☆ Tip
Look for spider skins shed as they grow. Try garden sheds or old webs. They are good to draw as they don't move.

☆ Tip
A magnifying glass is useful so that you can look closely at your subject and draw detail that would otherwise be invisible.

Stag beetles

These magnificent, harmless insects look like miniature aliens. Don't miss a chance to draw a live one or you might find a specimen in a museum.

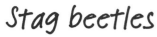 **Key point**

Always make several drawings from different viewpoints, not just one.

Drawing tool

A dip pen makes an exciting line. You could also use a sharpened feather.

Tracing paper rubbed with wax crayon

Graph paper

Newspaper partly covered with white.

 *Insect life*

Use your sketchbook to draw these creatures. This will help you understand how they move and what it is about them that is scary. It will be very useful when you are making up imaginary monsters. Prepare your sketchbook with different surfaces (see page 65). Make notes as well as drawings. Note their size and colour, how shiny they are and so on.

Dinosaurs

These terrifying-looking beasts are another kind of real-life monster.

👁 Observe

You can gradually build your drawing up from two different-sized ovals. Notice its small arms. No-one really knows what purpose they served.

Tyrannosaurus rex

Shape

It is the T. rex's massive build that makes it so frightening, so make sure its legs and body are thick and sturdy. Its head is huge in proportion to its body.

Pterodactyl

These bird-like flying reptiles look great against a dramatic sky.
As your confidence grows, experiment with different wing positions. Watch real live birds to learn how wings open and fold.

Drawing tool

I drew these dinosaurs with colouring pencils. See also page 88.

Shape

The basic shape of this Stegosaurus can be adapted to many different kinds of dinosaur. With a longer neck and tail it can be turned into an Apatosaurus or Diplodocus. Shorter front legs and a larger head could make it into a Camptosaurus.

Stegosaurus

Colour

It is impossible to know the colour and patterns of these monsters. What would have been useful? Were they camouflaged to merge in with their habitat or were they highly coloured to be easily seen by others of their kind? Use your imagination.
It would help to visit a zoo and study some living reptiles like lizards (see also pages 118-121).

People Monsters

The starting point for all the monsters on this page is the human form, so it will help to practise drawing people in your sketchbook. Start with stick people, then build up your drawing.

Vampire

Observe

This vampire is really a man in a suit. Only his fangs give him away, although the cloak and slicked-back hair help give him a sinister air. To make the vampire look humorous, draw the fangs as big as you like.

Colour

Make the inside of the vampire's cloak red for a dramatic effect.

Here is a classic sequence of boy to monster.

👁 Observe

Werewolves change from men to wolves at full moon. They have faces with the characteristics of both animals. Look at photographs of wolves for the nose and eyes but keep the basic arrangements of features as for a man.

Werewolf

👁 Observe

Notice how in the early stages the changes are minimal: the hair first, then one eye and the teeth in stage 3. Even when the transformation is complete, the boy monster still wears the same clothes.

Making the shadow bigger and bigger gives this sequence more drama.

Dead-people Monsters

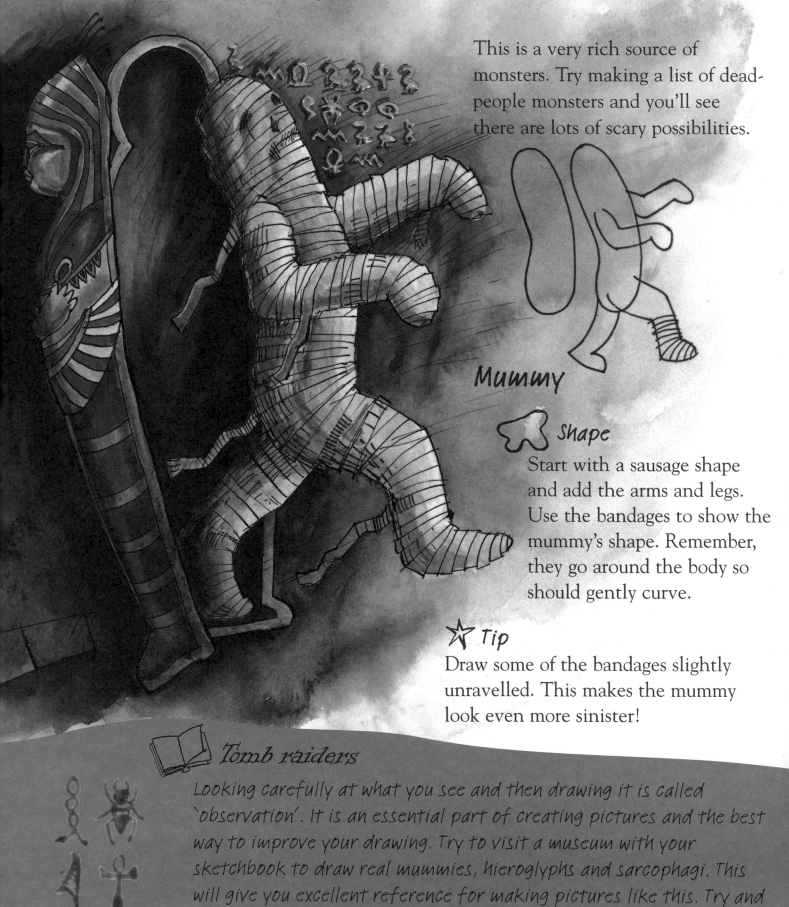

This is a very rich source of monsters. Try making a list of dead-people monsters and you'll see there are lots of scary possibilities.

Mummy

Shape

Start with a sausage shape and add the arms and legs. Use the bandages to show the mummy's shape. Remember, they go around the body so should gently curve.

☆ Tip

Draw some of the bandages slightly unravelled. This makes the mummy look even more sinister!

Tomb raiders

Looking carefully at what you see and then drawing it is called 'observation'. It is an essential part of creating pictures and the best way to improve your drawing. Try to visit a museum with your sketchbook to draw real mummies, hieroglyphs and sarcophagi. This will give you excellent reference for making pictures like this. Try and come home with a sketchbook full of notes, drawings and research.

Ghosts

These bubble-like ghosts are great fun to draw and not difficult.

Drawing tool

Use colour carefully. These ghosts are almost transparent, so you need a light, delicate touch. Watercolour or felt-pens washed over with water are ideal.

☆ Tip

Match the colour of the background in your ghost. This makes it extra-eerie!

Frankenstein's Monster

Shape

This monster will look convincing if you get the proportions right. Notice the huge forehead and long arms.

☆ Tip

Frankenstein's Monster was put together out of lots of bits, so remember to show the stitching. This picture was done with collage to give the right effect.

Ghoul

Half Human Monsters

There are many monsters that are combinations of humans and different animals. To make really convincing drawings, practise drawing people and the relevant animal before trying to put them together in one creature.

Mono-print Medusa

For the drawing of Medusa opposite, I have used a process known as mono-print. It is perfect for making this scary and smudgy portrait. It is called a mono-print because unlike most ways of print-making this only makes *one* image.

You will need a piece of perspex, black oil paint and a brush or roller.

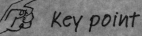 **Key point**
Use oil paint because it dries slowly so the paper doesn't stick to the glass if you take a long time drawing. Be careful not to put on too much paint.

Cover the perspex with the paint. Use a brush or roller.

Lay your paper on to the painted surface and press it down lightly.

Draw Medusa on the back of the paper with a sharp pencil.

Tips

a. Notice how the brush marks you make when painting the perspex are visible in the finished print. Use this to your advantage and 'draw' with the paint when putting it on the perspex.

b. To keep areas of the print white put pieces of paper between the painted perspex and the paper.

c. For a lighter print, press a piece of newspaper on to the painted perspex first. This will remove excess paint.

d. For dark areas rub hard with your fingers on the back of the paper.

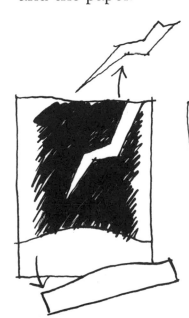 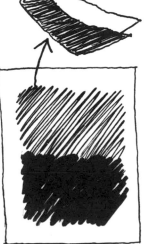 

Minotaur

In ancient Greek mythology, the Minotaur was half-bull and half-man and lived in the Labyrinth at Knossos.

Key point

When you make two different creatures into one, take one characteristic of the animal and draw it over the whole monster. So I have covered the Minotaur in the bull's fur and dotted the fish scales all over the Siren. This helps make the creature look whole.

Centaur

Half-man and half-horse.

Practise drawing horses and men first.

Siren

Not all monsters are hideous. The Sirens were half-bird and half-mermaid and sang so beautifully from their rocky island that sailors forgot everything. They even forgot to eat and so died of hunger!

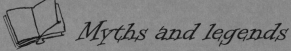

Myths and legends

If you put these creatures in their background, it helps create the right exciting and dramatic atmosphere. So read the myths and legends (Greek, Roman and Norse) and make notes in your sketchbook. Use the extra details in your drawings.

☆ Tip

Either follow these step-by-step drawings or you could make a collage using pictures of both creatures cut from magazines. It may take time to find two pictures that fit together well. Then try drawing your collage creatures.

☆ Tip

The Siren's scales should overlap like this.

Plant Monsters

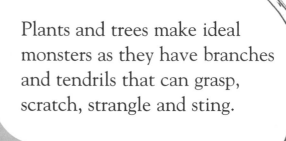

 Beansprouts

1. Curl a piece of blotting paper round the inside of a glass.
2. Stuff the middle with kitchen towel.
3. Place a bean between the glass and the blotting paper. (The kitchen towel should stop the bean slipping down.)
4. Fill the glass about a quarter full of water and keep it topped-up.
5. Make a drawing each day. The bean will grow slowly at first but soon so fast that you may wish to make two drawings a day.

Plants and trees make ideal monsters as they have branches and tendrils that can grasp, scratch, strangle and sting.

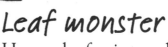 **Key point**

Basing your drawings on real plants will make them very believable. This is a drawing of a real Venus Flytrap. The only part of it that is invented are the eyes.

Leaf monster

Here a leaf print makes the body for this monster. Experiment with different leaves.

Key point

The best possible way to improve your drawing is to draw directly from observation (looking carefully).

Plants and trees are perfect for this as they are everywhere and they don't move.

This Triffid-like monster shoots poisonous pollen!

Tree monsters

Old and gnarled trees drawn at night need little adding to turn them into frightening monsters. Use the bark and the grain in the wood to create features. Turn branches into claw-like fingers!

Giants

Giants can be friendly and good or mean and bad. The important thing when drawing them is to make sure that they look seriously big.

Key point

To emphasise the giant's size, make the background tiny. Or only show a part of him, say just an enormous pair of feet.

Tip

Look at the short sleeves and trousers. If he is slightly too big for his clothes, he'll seem even bigger.

Shape

Notice how I've made this giant slightly hunched. This helps imply how tall he is, as he is always having to bend under things.

The Cyclops

These were a group of three giants who only had one eye each in the centre of their forehead. Their names were Steropes, Brontes and Arges and their job was to forge iron.

 **Key point**

We are emphasising the size of this cyclops because we are looking at him from an ant's-eye viewpoint. Rather like a towering skyscraper, look how he gets smaller as we look up into his staring face!

Talus

Talus was an enormous giant made of brass. He would heat himself up by lying in a fire and then rush forward to hug his enemies to his chest, so both squeezing and burning them to death!

☆ **Tip**

Talus was made of brass so make your lines angular. This will help make him look hard like metal.

 Colour

Add orange round Talus to give the impression that he is glowing.

Ogres

Ogres are a kind of giant with a *very* nasty character.

Smaller left eye and ear for a really wicked look.

Bushy frowning eyebrows. (Ogres are usually cross.)

Colour
Use dark, moody colours to help him look sinister.

Goggle gremlin

INKY IMP

SPLAT spectre

Aargh

Inky ogres

Splash some ink on to paper and stare at it. Can you see any shape or face? This is a really good way of creating monsters as ink blots can nearly always be turned into something. Gradually add eyes or mouths full of sharp teeth or whatever you like. You can blow the ink around by using a straw. That's a good way of creating grotesque arms and legs.

Trolls

Trolls can be big one-eyed giants or small mischievous dwarves. They can have horns, lots of arms and be covered in scales. Most have long white hair.

👁 Observe
I've given this troll a snout-like nose and a wide grin. Although sly, trolls are often believed to be slow-witted so these characteristics help to create this impression.

👆 Key point
As with the ogre, I've given this troll one small eye and one big eye. This helps to give him a slightly suspicious air. He looks as if he is up to no good, and WHAT is he holding behind his back?

Dragons

The word dragon comes from the Greek 'drakon' which means 'to see' and 'to watch'. When we think of dragons we usually think of them as serpents who never sleep, guarding huge hordes of treasure.

👁 Observe

This dragon, curled round his gold, is roughly egg-shaped. Gradually add details of the body, neck and head. Use curved rings around the tail and neck to make the dragon look three-dimensional.

Key point

A dragon is very like a crocodile so it will really help you to draw dragons if you look at photographs of crocodiles. Better still, go and visit a zoo to draw live crocodiles, iguanas and other large lizards.

This dragon's spiny neck and tail were based on drawings of lizards I made at London Zoo.

Tip

You may want to cover your dragon with scales so look back at the Siren on page 77.

Dragon's hoard

You can see images of dragons everywhere: on coins, flags and coats-of-arms; as stone sculptures on castles; and as logos on packaging. Keep a drawing record in your sketchbook of as many dragons as you can find. Try preparing your sketchbook pages with patches of fiery colours to draw on. Save foil and sweet papers and stick these down to create a glittering metal surface for your dragons. Draw with a ball-point pen, wax crayon or oil pastel.

Aliens

This really is a chance to let your imagination run wild as an alien might look like almost anything. Here is a selection of aliens to start you off but try to create your own as well.

👁 Observe
This *War of the Worlds*-type alien resembles both a spider and a skull and looks very scary.

☆ Tip
Many aliens are based on machines and robots so try to visit a science museum with your sketchbook.

📖 Cosmic creatures
Look through magazines and cut out scraps like eyes, animals, machinery or whatever takes your fancy. Now arrange the scraps in your sketchbook to create alien beings, the more bizarre the better. Finally make drawings from your collage creatures. You could invent a picture fact-file for them: show them eating, playing or fighting.

Shape

Start with half a sphere. Remember it is three-dimensional. Draw in the bottom section and add the skull-like eyes and nose cavity. Finally add the tripod legs to make this monster walk.

Observe

This rather insect-like alien looks like a predator. I was inspired by some drawings I had of a praying mantis and they form the basis of this monster. Can you recognize any other insects in him?

Observe

The little cluster of shapes at the end of the body hint at wings. Maybe this alien can fly!

Tip

The use of strong shadows make this picture very dramatic. Placing the frightened earthlings here creates the impression that they are already beyond help.

Many-headed Monsters

⭐ **Tip**

You could also draw all the heads separately. Cut them out and stick everything together. If you can photocopy the finished result no-one will know you did it!

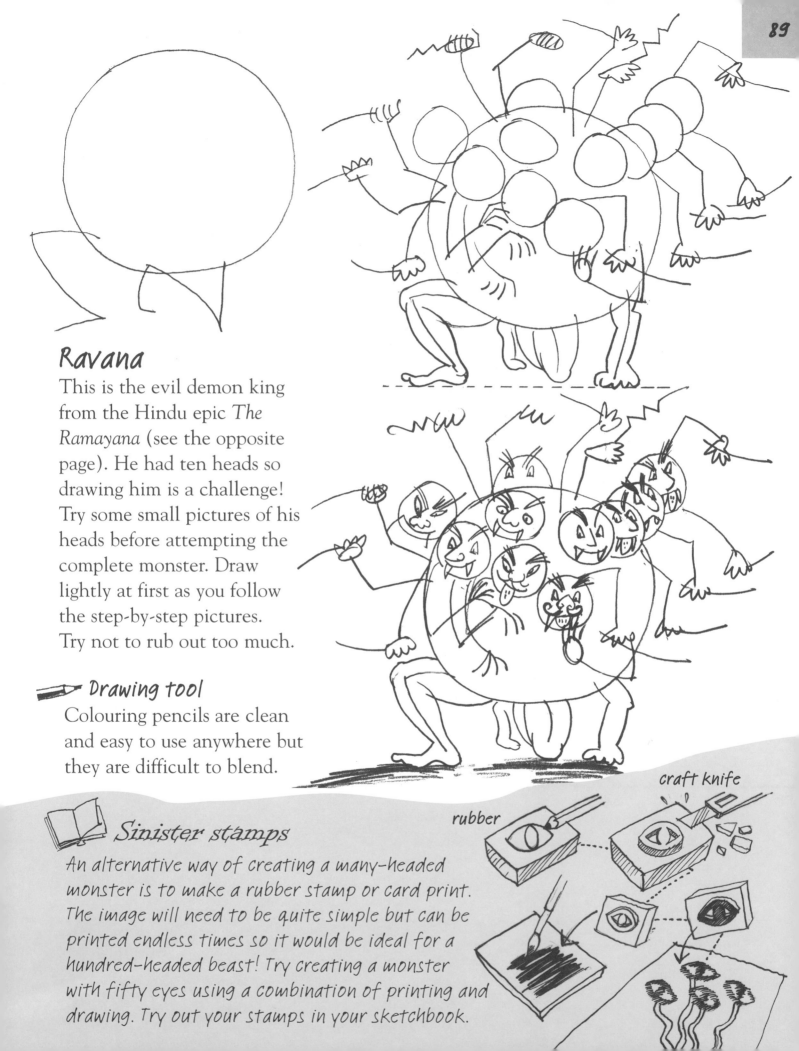

Ravana

This is the evil demon king from the Hindu epic *The Ramayana* (see the opposite page). He had ten heads so drawing him is a challenge! Try some small pictures of his heads before attempting the complete monster. Draw lightly at first as you follow the step-by-step pictures. Try not to rub out too much.

Drawing tool

Colouring pencils are clean and easy to use anywhere but they are difficult to blend.

Sinister stamps

An alternative way of creating a many-headed monster is to make a rubber stamp or card print. The image will need to be quite simple but can be printed endless times so it would be ideal for a hundred-headed beast! Try creating a monster with fifty eyes using a combination of printing and drawing. Try out your stamps in your sketchbook.

rubber

craft knife

More Many-headed Monsters

The Lernean Hydra

A snake-like monster in Greek mythology, some say it had one hundred heads. Others say nine but every time Hercules cut one off, two sprang up in its place!

Key point

Don't be put off having a go at drawing this monster because it looks too difficult. Drawing one head will be practice for the rest.

Shape

Look how all nine heads have similar features. Start with the head, a squashed-egg shape. Add the mouth which almost divides the head in half, then the eyes and arching eye sockets. The long necks get gradually thicker as they join the body.

Drawing tool

This drawing was made with a soft pencil. Notice how the shading helps us see the drawing more clearly. The dark areas show us the shape of the body and stop us getting confused by all of the hydra's heads.

The lines going round the tail and body help make this monster look solid and three-dimensional.

Sea Monsters

Krakens, Leviathans and sea serpents are monsters of the sea from classical myths. For centuries sailors have terrified us with their tales of fabulous beasts of the sea.

Here are some sea monsters for you to copy. Notice how their basic shape is similar. The neck and head rise out of the sea, as does the tail. Try creating your own sea monsters, using this as a foundation.

Fathoms-deep fish

Unbelievably, we are still discovering new species of fish that live deep, deep down at the bottom of the ocean. They are bizarre and fascinating creatures and can be seen in books or on TV. Make studies of these deep-sea fish in your sketchbook.
Try drawing them in white on a black background. You can use a collection of drawings like this as a starting point for sea monsters.

Look for spouting whales and writhing sea serpents on old maps and charts. Add drawings of them to your sketchbook.

Key point

Study and draw real fish to help you achieve convincing details. You can buy fish from a fish shop or supermarket. Look at how the scales overlap and how the fins are attached. This is all part of your research and an essential part of learning to draw well.

Believe it or not Monsters

Here is a double-page spread of real-life mysteries. They might really exist as there are fuzzy photographs of all of these monsters!

Abominable Snowman (or Yeti)

The Yeti lives high up in the snowy Himalayas so we might imagine it to have thick white fur.

The Loch Ness Monster

Try drawing the Loch Ness Monster in a misty, murky lake.

☆ Tip
You might find it easier to draw all of Nessie rather than just what is above the water. Then rub out the lower parts.

Observe

The Yeti and Bigfoot are quite similar as they are both ape-like monsters. Look how gorilla-like their faces are and, if you get the opportunity to draw gorillas at the zoo, this would be excellent practice.

Bigfoot

The Bigfoot has been sighted in the Canadian forests of Saskatchewan and photographs show it as a dark brown or black.

Drawing all these monsters in their natural surroundings helps persuade us that they may really exist.

Top Ten Tips

⭐ Use strong shadows to create drama.

⭐ Show part of a monster. It can sometimes be more scary than drawing all of it.

⭐ Give your monster a name. It can help trigger your imagination, e.g. Creepy Crimson Crab Eater.

⭐ The more you draw the better you will get. So practise, practise, practise.

⭐ Think where your monster lives. It may help you imagine what it looks like.

⭐ Draw from life. It will help you draw everything, not just monsters.

⭐ Always keep a sketchbook with you and draw at every available opportunity.

⭐ Practise drawing your monster from different viewpoints, and not just once.

⭐ Add written sound effects to your drawings. It can help bring them to life.

⭐ Most of all, enjoy your drawing.

GOOD LUCK!

Wild Animals

Introduction

This part of the book is to help you to draw and paint wild animals and there are many different ways to do this. You can use the step-by-step drawing guides which encourage you to study the animal's size, shape and detail, and there are pages of animal drawings for you to copy. There are useful tips for drawing animals at the zoo and at the museum and ideas for sketchbook practice.
But the most important thing is to **enjoy drawing**.

 ## *Making a sketchbook*

A great way to get better at drawing is to keep a sketchbook. All good artists do this. You can buy one or just as easily make one by clipping pieces of paper together. In either case, it is a good idea to prepare each double page by giving it a background. Look at the suggestions below. It is fun to draw on these surfaces and they will help you make really interesting drawings. (Notice that some of the drawings in this book use prepared backgrounds too.) Look for the symbol for sketchbook ideas.

tea

white paint

brown paper

grey wash

old packaging lightly painted over with white

patches of colour

gumstrip

Lions

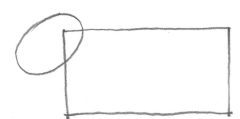

👁 Observe

Look carefully at a lion. If you can't get to a zoo (see page 111), then look at this lion.

(see page 111)

👉 Key points

I usually begin with the eyes. Notice how drawing in the patches of white around the eyes really helps your drawing to look like a lion. Also the lines of black dots beneath the nose are important details.

〰 Shape

The lion's body is roughly rectangular in shape so it might help if you sketch this in first.

Lions and tigers are members of the cat family. So if you look at and draw a cat, this will also help you to draw lions and tigers.

Colour

Almost half of my lion is covered by his shaggy mane which is made up of many different shades of yellow and brown – not just one colour.

★ Tip

Don't forget to draw the lion's ear, almost hidden in his mane.

Drawing tool

This lion is drawn with a 2B pencil. Pencil will give you many different shades and tones, from almost black to pale grey. The softer the pencil, the greater the variety of tones.

Lion hunt!

Lions appear on many different products and packaging. Try recording these in a sketchbook. You can copy them or stick in pictures. How many can you find?

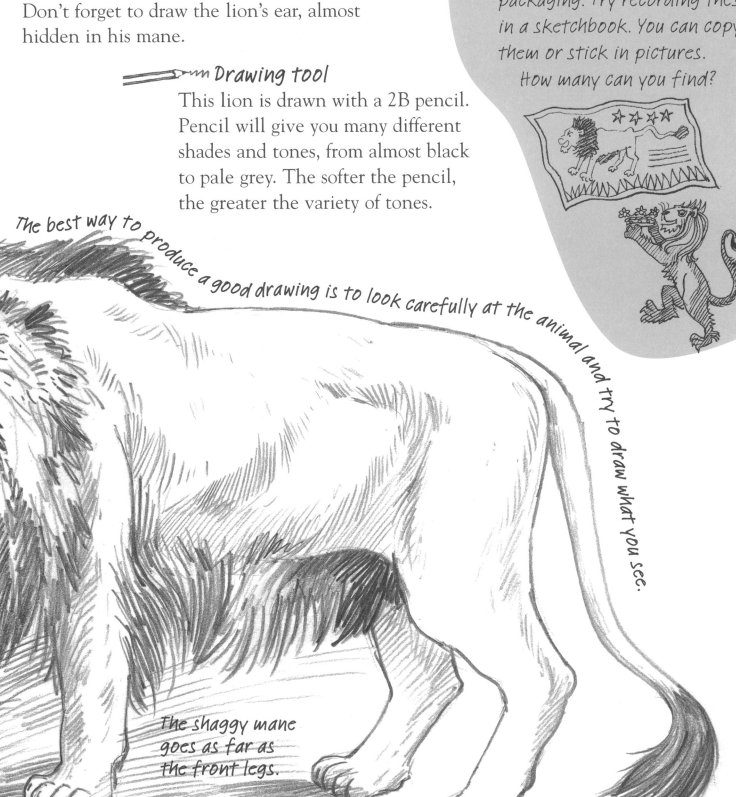

The best way to produce a good drawing is to look carefully at the animal and try to draw what you see.

The shaggy mane goes as far as the front legs.

More Big Cats

The most important features of a tiger are its stripes and beautiful orange colour.
Look at the pattern made by the orange and white fur on the tiger's face and body.
If you can get this right it will make all the difference.
No two tigers have exactly the same pattern so look really carefully.

Here are two pages full of lions and tigers and other big cats.
Practise copying them. You could also try to draw them in a landscape.

⭐ SPECIAL TIP!
The best practice of all is to draw animals from life, so this probably means a visit to the zoo (see page 111).

Spanish Lynx

Tiger

Cheetah

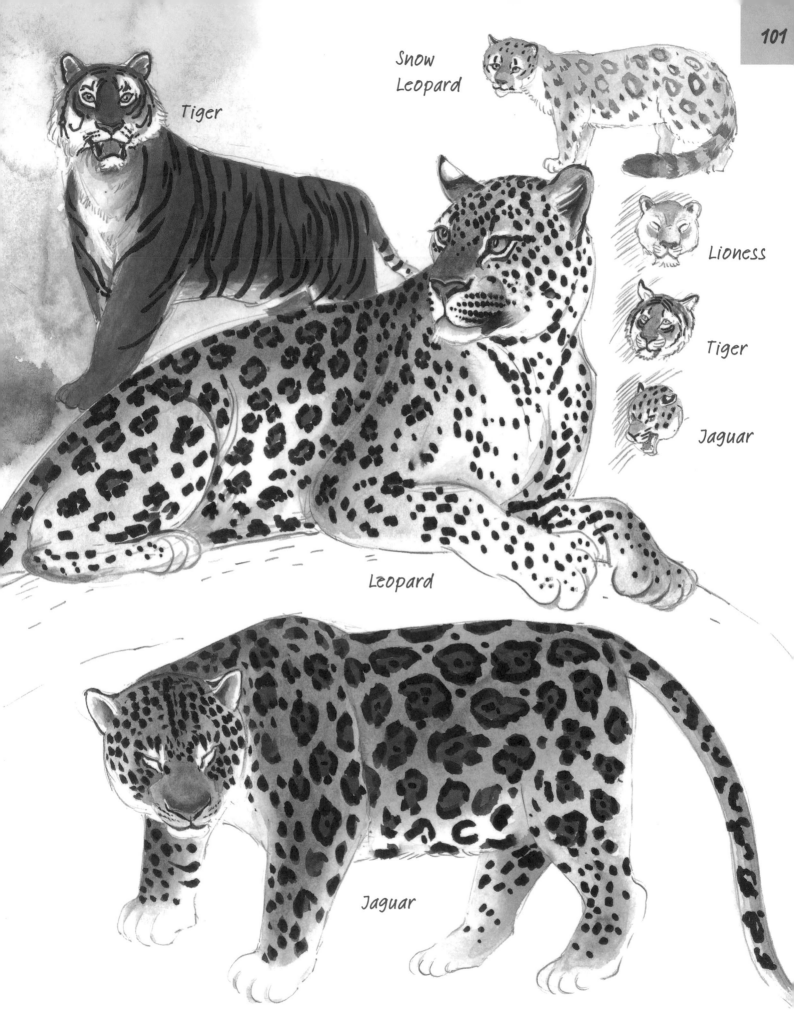

Tiger

Snow Leopard

Lioness

Tiger

Jaguar

Leopard

Jaguar

Notice how the jaguar is heavily built and has marks inside the spots, unlike the leopard.

Brown Bears

Shape

An oval will give you a shape for the body and the neck. The head is very roughly a rectangle.

⭐ Tip

Draw lightly to start with and gradually 'flesh out' your drawing adding the features.

Key point

Notice how the highest point is the Brown Bear's shoulder. This is very characteristic and will help make your drawing look right. Draw a line from the peak of the shoulder downwards to give you the position of the front paw.

Making your mark

Draw a series of squares in your sketchbook and practise filling in each with different marks. You could use a pencil, pen, brush, or chalk. The more varied the marks you make, the more you will increase your chance of producing a good drawing. Look at the range of pencil marks used to draw the Brown Bear's fur. Sketchbook exercises like this really improve your skill in handling materials.

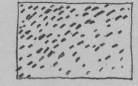

Observe

Notice how the shaggy fur helps to show the animal's form.

Drawing tool

All these bears are drawn with a 4B pencil. This gives a good range of tones for fur.

Polar Bears

These magnificent bears are now rarely seen in zoos, so you could draw them at a museum, or even from a film. This is a challenge, but great fun – and, as a last resort, there is always the pause button!

Fish

Fish in an aquarium are great fun to draw. They are constantly moving but you'll find that they often return to the same position so you have an excellent chance to draw them well.

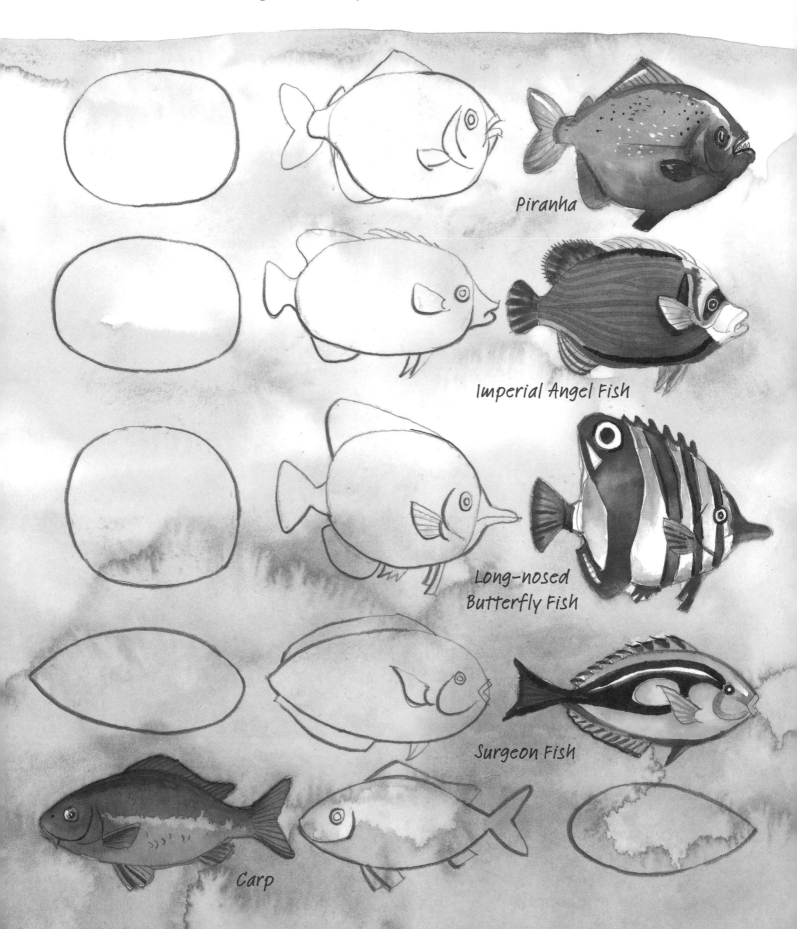

Piranha

Imperial Angel Fish

Long-nosed Butterfly Fish

Surgeon Fish

Carp

 Observe

Look carefully at the fish. They may be different shapes and sizes but they all have gills, fins, two eyes and a tail.

 Shape

Draw in the basic shape LIGHTLY. Add the fins, gill, tail, and the eye.

 Colour

These fish are beautiful because of their varied colours and patterns. Enjoy adding these details.

Key point

Try to make your colours dazzle and sparkle as they do on the marine fish. Felt-pens used with water are ideal (see Parrots, page 108).

☆ Tip

Be careful – some fish, like the Long-nosed Butterfly Fish, have a false eye to frighten enemies. Don't be fooled!

Drawing from life

A fishmonger gave me these fish heads, so I could make careful, detailed drawings of them. This is called 'observational drawing' and certainly helps you to draw better. Ask a grown-up to buy you a fish from a fish shop. Then you can try some observational drawings in your sketchbook. Remember, prepare your sketchbook first.

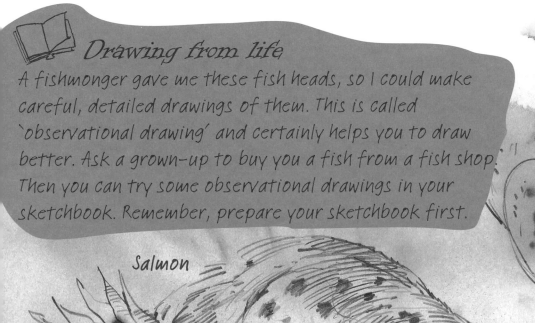

Salmon

Plaice

Mackerel

 Drawing tool

This paper was prepared by washing it in coffee! You can also use watercolour for the bright fish. See page 121.

Birds

Whether you live in the countryside or the town you will probably be surrounded by birds. Once you have mastered the basic shape, you should manage to draw any species and there are thousands to choose from.

If you put out scraps regularly for birds not too far from a window, you will have ready subjects to draw. You need to see clearly and be able to draw in comfort without disturbing the birds.

Eagle Owl

Shape

A small rectangle is a good base for the head. Make the sides of this rectangle bulge outward – this will help with the shape. Find the centre of the rectangle and this will give you a guide for the beak and eyes. A large oval is ideal for the body.

Falcon head

 Key point

It is the markings on the Peregrine Falcon that really make this bird recognisable. Try practising the falcon's head and plumage (feathers) in your sketchbook.

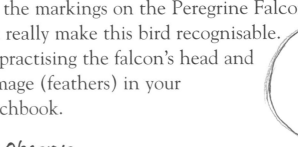

Mallard

 Observe

Notice how adding the 'eyebrows' gives this falcon his angry bird-of-prey stare.

☆ **Tip**

Draw as lightly as you can at first, then darken your pencil line when you are sure it is correct.

Peregrine Falcon

On the spot

Try taking your sketchbook to a park where there are ducks. You'll find the ducks are used to people being around and so are quite tame. This kind of 'location' drawing is the best possible kind of practice. Look carefully at your subject and draw what you see.

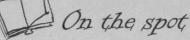

Parrots

For the main shape of the parrot, use the step-by-step drawings in Birds, page 106.

Puffin

 Drawing tool

Felt-pens are great for bright, brilliant colour. So they are perfect for drawing these very colourful and noisy birds.

Crossbill

African Grey Parrot

Use felt-pens to colour small areas of the bird.

Then use a wet brush to spread the ink around and colour the whole bird.

Wait for the colour to dry and then add the final details with the felt-pens.

Avocet

☆ Tip
BE CAREFUL - don't use too much water, a little goes a long way.

Red and Blue Macaw

Spoonbill

Flamingo

 Beak collection

There are many different types of birds with many different types of beaks, each adapted to suit the needs of its owner. Try drawing a collection of different beaks in your sketchbook.

Long-billed Iiwi

* Only one bird out of the many thousands of species has a beak with the top half much shorter than the bottom half.

Can you see it here?

Skimmer

The last colour I added to these toucans was black as it runs easily into the other colours and smudges them.

Keel-Billed Toucan

Red Breasted Toucan

Toco Toucan

Scarlet Macaw

Hyacinthine Macaws

Here are some tropical birds for you to copy. Try to capture their bright and brilliant colours. Use the technique described on the opposite page.

Elephants

Elephants are the largest living land animals but are surprisingly quiet. Notice how careful and precise their movements are. Try to capture this when you draw them.

 ## Observe

Look carefully at an elephant.

Shape

A large oval tilting downwards with a smaller circle at the top end will give you the basic shape. The trunk unfolded will reach to the ground. Look carefully at the bumps on the elephant's head. They are important and will help make your drawing convincing. As always, the key to success is looking and noticing.

Key point

This is an Asiatic Elephant. It has smaller ears than its African cousin and an arched back. It also has four toenails on each back foot – an African elephant only has three.

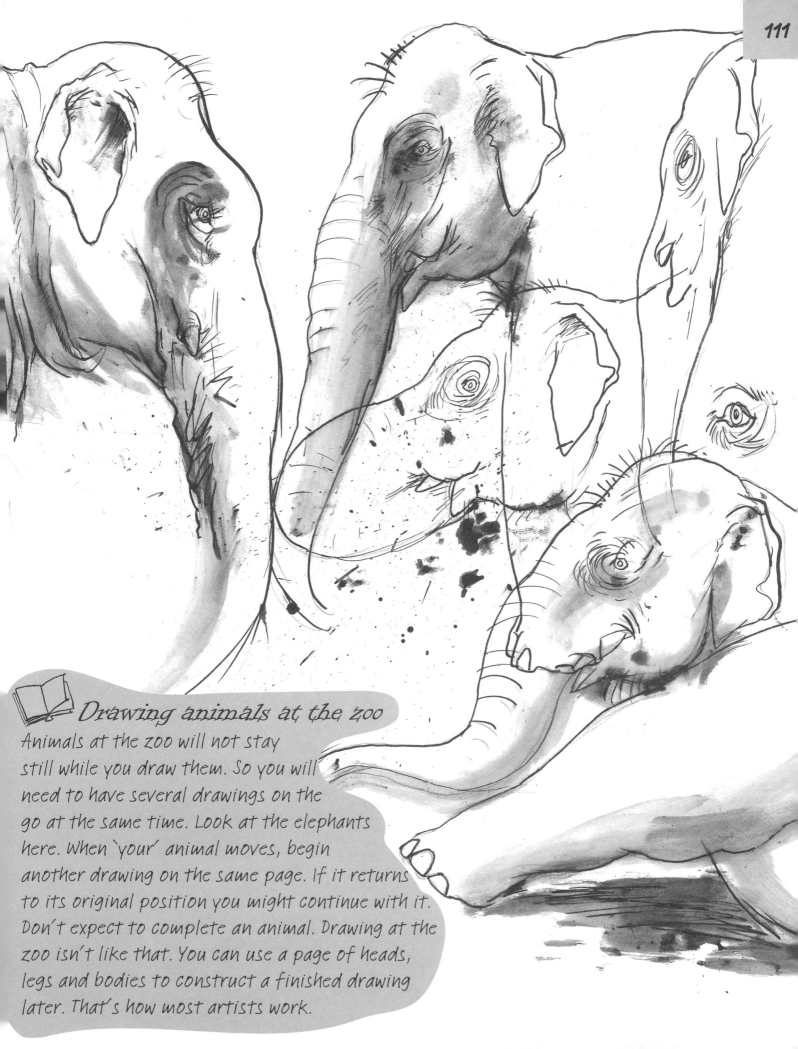

📖 *Drawing animals at the zoo*

Animals at the zoo will not stay still while you draw them. So you will need to have several drawings on the go at the same time. Look at the elephants here. When `your´ animal moves, begin another drawing on the same page. If it returns to its original position you might continue with it. Don't expect to complete an animal. Drawing at the zoo isn't like that. You can use a page of heads, legs and bodies to construct a finished drawing later. That's how most artists work.

Deer and Antelope

These animals are graceful and very beautiful.
Whatever their size, the basic shape is the same
for any of the huge variety of species of antelope.
The tiny Royal Antelope is no bigger than a
rabbit, yet the Moose can be nearly 2.5 metres
tall at the shoulder, taller than a very tall
basketball player!

White-tail Deer

Springbok

👁 Observe
Look at this White-tail Deer.

🐾 Shape
A rectangle for the body and a circle for the head will start you off. Remember – draw lightly at first and gradually strengthen your drawing when you are happy that it's accurate.

👆 Key point
This White-tail Deer is leaping through the forest. Try to capture something of its energy and life in this pose. Your White-tail Deer should look as if it has leapt onto the page and may just leap off again. The quick pen drawings of Impala attempt to do just that.

Impala

Bongo

Topi

Brindle Gnu

Blackbuck

Dama Gazelle

Chital Deer

📖 Head hunting

See how many species of deer and antelope you can find. Look in books, magazines, museums, zoos and parks and on the television. Then just sketch a collection of heads, like this.

Langur Monkeys

Monkeys are lively and often fast moving.
This can make them difficult to draw from life.

👁 Observe

Look at this Langur. Notice his long arms, legs
and tail. He has five fingers and a thumb like us
but they are long and thin.

☞ Key point

The body is rather like an oval and the Langur's
head in proportion is quite small and square
(see detail on the opposite page). Noticing
things like this will make all the difference to
your drawing. Draw the arms, legs and tail in
with lines first, then add the details.

🖌 Drawing tool

Try using a ball-point pen or a fountain pen.
These are good tools for drawing quickly.

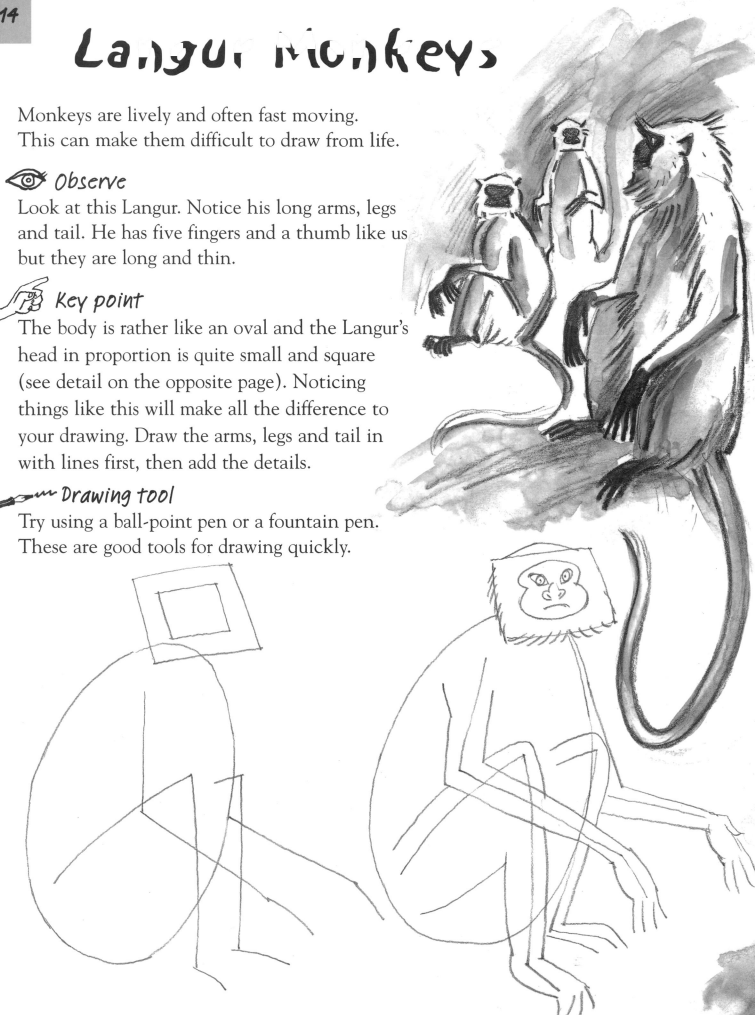

Langur head

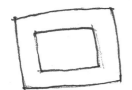

Shape

The Langur's face is square in shape and fringed with white fur. Try lightly drawing a square within a square to start you off. Then sketch in the shape of the face and the eyes, nose and mouth. Finally draw in the hair and shade in the darker face, ears and top of the head.

☆ Tip

Notice how the eyes are heavily shaded by the Langur's brow.

📖 Looks familiar

We have similar features to monkeys as you've probably noticed! So if you look in the mirror and draw your own face and hands in your sketchbook, this will help you to draw monkeys.

Langur

The Langur's fur is quite long and thick so add this at the end with your drawing tool!

More Apes and Monkeys

Here are some more members of the monkey family for you to copy.
The colour of their faces and pattern of their fur vary tremendously across
the huge variety of species BUT they all follow the same basic shape.

Mandrill

Squirrel Monkey

Spider Monkey

 *Print primates*

These monkeys belong to the Guenon family, so they all have a similar shape although different species have different markings. Try making a simple print. You can cut a simple monkey shape out of a piece of lino, a potato, or a piece of card as I have done here. Using this as a stamp I filled in their markings and patterns when I visited a natural history museum. It makes an exciting identification chart. Use the same idea for other animal species.

Guenons

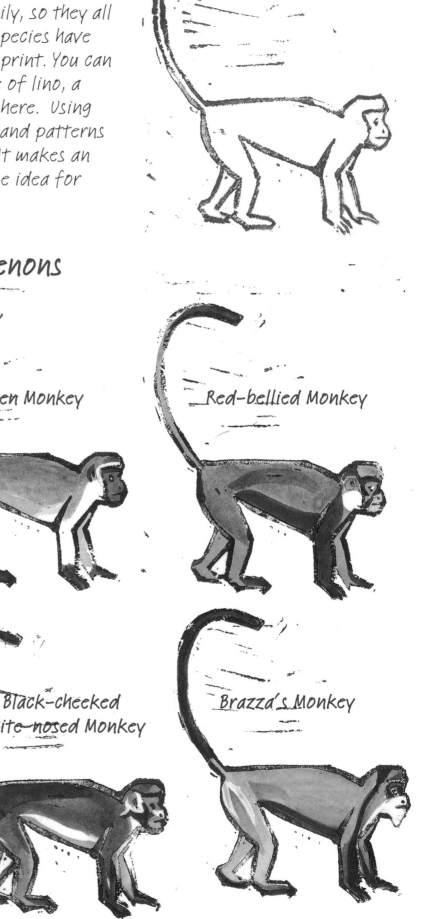

Diana Monkey

Green Monkey

Red-bellied Monkey

Blue Monkey

Black-cheeked White-nosed Monkey

Brazza's Monkey

Reptiles and Amphibians

Reptiles often spend long periods without moving, especially if they are cold. So they are perfect subjects to draw from life. Even if they do move, they very often return to their original position so there really is the chance for a close look.

Observe

Like living dragons, iguanas are really members of the reptile family. Look at them carefully. They are lizards and share many similarities with geckos, skinks and even crocodiles.

Drawing tool

Here I have used a pencil but for the two iguanas at the bottom of page 119, I used a dip pen. It is the perfect tool for these spiky lizards.

Shape

An egg shape and a larger oval will give you the basic shape. The tail can be indicated with a line. This will ensure that all of your iguana fits on the page. A smaller egg shape inside the first one will give you a guide for the left eye. The bump of the right eye will be parallel. Draw in the flap of skin under the chin and the bump of the iguana's neck.

First sketch in the arms and legs and later 'flesh them out'. The left hind leg is hidden in this drawing and we can only see the hand of the left arm.

Key point

The scales and spikes show the iguana's shape. The stripes running round the body and tail also help to make it look solid and three-dimensional. Notice how the stripes show the curve of the body – this is really important.

Iguana

⭐ *Tip*
The patterns on an animal's body
often help to show the shape.

More Reptiles

👁 Observe

The large bulging eyes and long arms and legs with spatula finger-tips are typical of all frogs.

Mouth-breeder Frog

Arrow-poison Frog (seven times larger than life!)

✏ Drawing tool

Most of the frogs on this page are Arrow-poison Frogs. They have very bright colours, so use felt-pen or watercolour (see opposite). I used colouring pencils for the Mouth-breeder Frog above. These are clean and easy to use but difficult to blend.

📖 Reptile reference

Make a concertina of reptiles and amphibians to fold out of your sketchbook. Use pictures from magazines and newspapers. This is an excellent way to build up a store of reference ready to use at any time.

Here are lots of reptiles and amphibians for you to copy. This will be good practice when you draw them from life. Look at the similarities between them. Drawing one will help you to draw another.

Drawing tool
Watercolour can be mixed to get exactly the right shade. To blend the colours on the page, work quickly while the colour is wet.

Gecko

Green Mamba

☆ **Tip**
Don't try to draw every scale on the snake. Use them to show the shape.

Camels and Zebras

Camels

Camels are curious animals to draw, with their strange legs and humps. They are good to draw from life as they usually move slowly.

👁 Observe

Look at a camel carefully.

Shape

Try drawing an egg shape for the head and an oval for the body. The thick fur on the camel's neck makes it appear to bulge outwards. Draw this in. Gradually build up your drawing following the steps here.

✋ Key point

Obviously the camel's humps are a vital feature. This is a Bactrian camel with two humps. The Arabian camel has one hump and is often wrongly called the Dromedary, which is in fact a special breed of one-humped camel used for riding.

Drawing tool

This finished drawing was made using a fountain pen. This is ideal for drawing on location. It doesn't dry up and can be smudged with water to show shadow.

Zebras

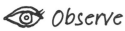 Observe

Look how the pattern of stripes on this zebra helps to show its shape.

Shape

Start by drawing an oval for the body and a smaller oval for the head. Remember to draw lightly at first. Gradually draw over these shapes, sketching in the form of the zebra.

Key point

Different species of zebra have different stripe patterns but, as a general rule, zebras from further north in Africa are more heavily striped than zebras from the south.

★ Tip

Draw in the stripes first before thickening them up.

Family matters

Remember that horses and zebras are very similar. A zebra gallops in exactly the same way as a horse. Try sketching ponies and you'll be well-prepared to draw zebras.

Lemurs

Aye-ayes

This strange and extremely rare animal is sometimes called 'The Witch's Cat' and it's easy to see why.

Observe

It has huge ears and eyes and a long bushy tail. But its strangest features are its very long, bony fingers, especially the middle finger which it uses to poke into holes looking for grubs.

Key point

The Aye-aye's tail is over three-fifths of its length, so leave enough room on your paper to fit it all in.

Shape

Build up your drawing from an oval and a triangle. Then work on the eyes and ears, its dominant features.

Animal notes

As one of the world's rarest mammals, the chance to draw this Aye-aye at London Zoo was wonderful. It was very dark in the Aye-aye house and the Aye-aye was constantly moving but you can learn a lot by just watching. Make written notes to jog your memory later. What does it do? Does it make a noise? How does it move?

Drawing tool

I used white acrylic to highlight the Aye-aye's long white hairs.

Ruffed Lemur

Black Lemur

Sifaka

Ring-tailed Lemur

Lemurs

Here are some other lemurs for you to copy. Try and find them at the zoo too.

Nocturnal Animals

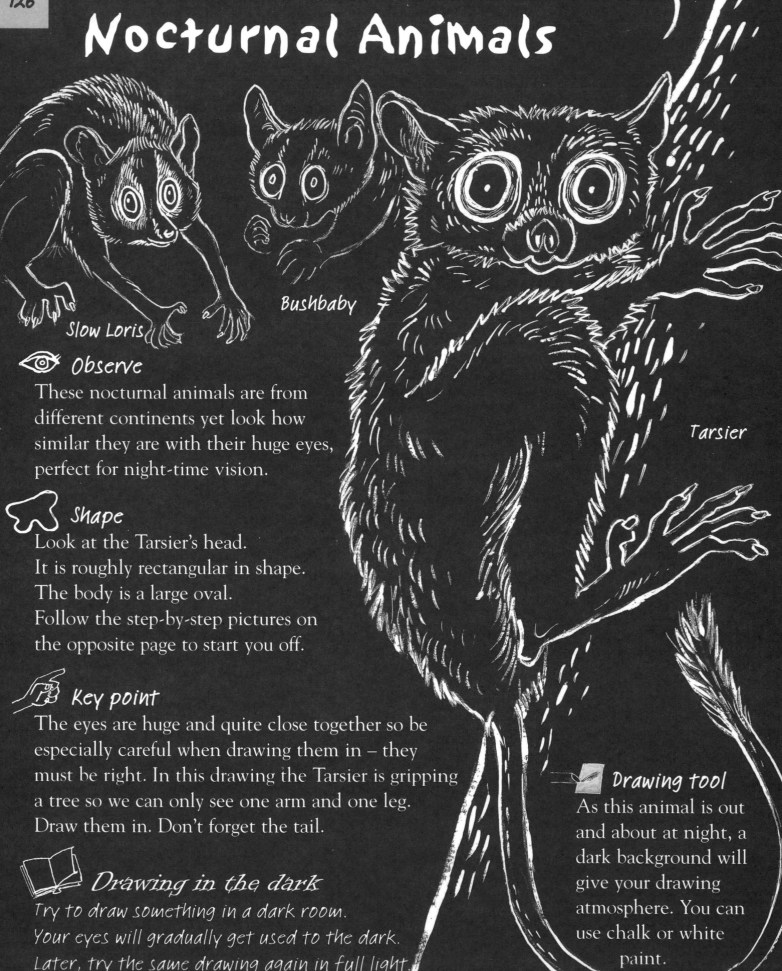

Slow Loris

Bushbaby

Tarsier

👁 Observe

These nocturnal animals are from different continents yet look how similar they are with their huge eyes, perfect for night-time vision.

Shape

Look at the Tarsier's head.
It is roughly rectangular in shape.
The body is a large oval.
Follow the step-by-step pictures on the opposite page to start you off.

Key point

The eyes are huge and quite close together so be especially careful when drawing them in – they must be right. In this drawing the Tarsier is gripping a tree so we can only see one arm and one leg. Draw them in. Don't forget the tail.

Drawing in the dark

Try to draw something in a dark room.
Your eyes will gradually get used to the dark.
Later, try the same drawing again in full light.

Drawing tool

As this animal is out and about at night, a dark background will give your drawing atmosphere. You can use chalk or white paint.

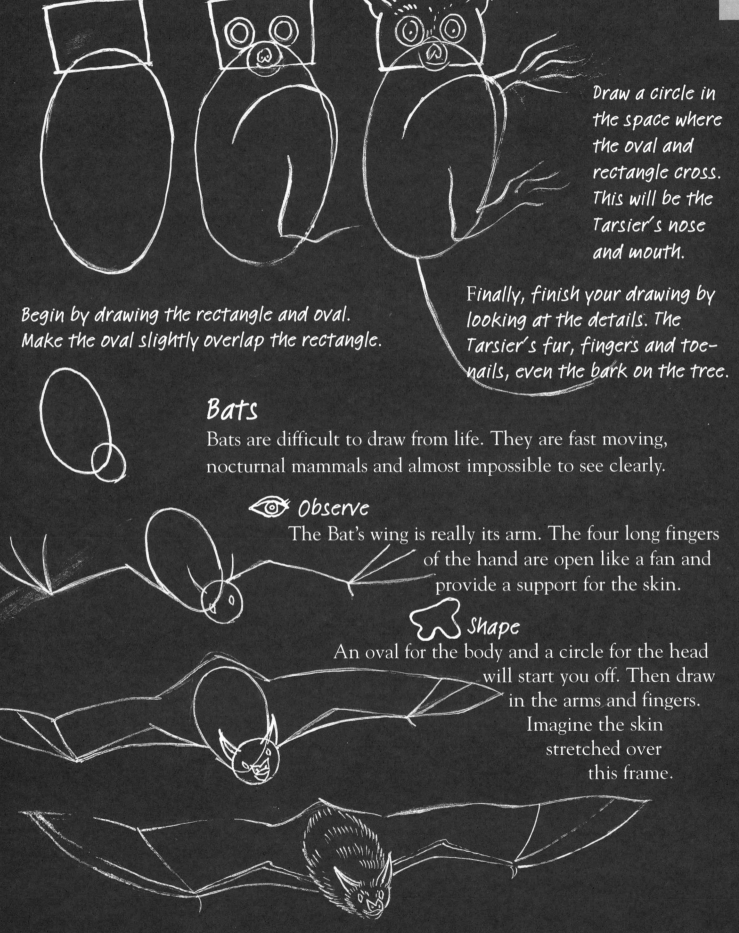

Draw a circle in the space where the oval and rectangle cross. This will be the Tarsier's nose and mouth.

Begin by drawing the rectangle and oval. Make the oval slightly overlap the rectangle.

Finally, finish your drawing by looking at the details. The Tarsier's fur, fingers and toe-nails, even the bark on the tree.

Bats

Bats are difficult to draw from life. They are fast moving, nocturnal mammals and almost impossible to see clearly.

👁 Observe

The Bat's wing is really its arm. The four long fingers of the hand are open like a fan and provide a support for the skin.

Shape

An oval for the body and a circle for the head will start you off. Then draw in the arms and fingers. Imagine the skin stretched over this frame.

Top Ten Tips

⭐ Try using lots of different implements to draw with.

⭐ When you draw with a pencil, make sure it's sharp. Pencils range from H = hard to B = soft. An HB pencil is exactly in the middle. For drawing wild animals you will always need an HB or softer. Never draw with a propelling pencil.

⭐ Use your eyes. Looking carefully at what you are drawing is essential.

⭐ Try not to rub out too much.

⭐ Practise and practise. The more you draw the better you will get.

⭐ Drawing an animal from life is the best possible practice.

⭐ Always carry your sketchbook with you – you never know when you might find something you want to draw.

⭐ Keep all your drawings. If you look at them after a period of time you will see them in a new light. They can often look better than you thought.

⭐ As well as drawing, make written notes. You can't draw the noise an animal makes but you can describe it.

⭐ Most of all, enjoy your drawing!

GOOD LUCK!